ST. LEGER: THE FAMILY AND THE RACE

Sir Ralph St. Leger, Sheriff of Kent, Constable of Leeds Castle, 1468, and Anne his wife.

ST. LEGER
The Family and the Race

Moya Frenz St. Leger

Publication sponsored by the
Janet A. Hooker Charitable Trust
in memory of her father
who loved Ireland and everything Irish

Phillimore

1986

Published by
PHILLIMORE & CO. LTD.
Shopwyke Hall, Chichester, Sussex

© Moya Frenz St. Leger, 1986

ISBN 0 85033 588 4

Printed and bound in Great Britain by
BILLING AND SON LIMITED
Worcester, England

CONTENTS

List of Plates vii
List of Text Illustrations ix
Acknowledgements xi

FIRST PART

1. 1066 and Some of That 1
2. A Wise and Warie Gentlemen 9
3. The Legacy 29
4. Doneraile 39

SECOND PART

5. The Race 63
6. The People of Park Hill 77
7. The American War 83
8. Poetry and Passion 92
9. The Old Saint 101
10. Nine Centuries On 109
11. The Right to Arms 125
    Epilogue 127
    Appendix One: Knights and Sheriffs 129
    Appendix Two: Members of Parliament 130
    Appendix Three: Manors and Lands in Kent 131
    Appendix Four: Two 16th-century letters 133
    Appendix Five: The Saint Legers of Kilkenny 135
    Appendix Six: Descendants of Sir Robert de St. Leger 139
    Appendix Seven: Descendants of the Lady Freemason ... 140
    Appendix Eight: St. Legers in Kent, 1619 142
    References and Notes 144
    Bibliography 148
    Index 151

LIST OF PLATES

(*between pages 82 and 83*)

1. Ulcombe Church
2. Sir Anthony St. Leger
3. The Ros tomb, St. George's Chapel, Windsor
4. Sir Richard Grenville
5. William Warham, Archbishop of Canterbury
6. Arms of Henry VIII, Catherine Parr, Sir Anthony St. Leger
7. Leeds Castle
8. John Philpot Curran
9. Doneraile Court
10. The Lady Castletown
11. Hayes St. Leger, 4th Viscount Doneraile
12. The 'oval field' at Park Hill
13. Doncaster Races, 1830
14. The Marquess of Rockingham
15. John Hayes St. Leger
16. John Hayes St. Leger
17. The Hon. Elizabeth St. Leger (as a girl)
18. The Hon. Mrs. Elizabeth Aldworth
19. Early *Cape Times* premises
20. *Cape Times* premises, 1978
21. Frederick York St. Leger, the 'Old Saint'
22. Grandfather Frederick York
23. At the German St. Leger, 1976
24. The author at the German St. Leger, 1976
25. Royal Crown Derby Commemorative Bicentenary Vase
26. St. Leger Stakes Bicentenary Commemorative Plate
27. Presentation of the Bicentenary Vase
28. Unveiling of plaque at the *Red Lion*, 1978
29. Today's grandstand at Doncaster
30. 'Find Anthony': a new inn sign

LIST OF TEXT ILLUSTRATIONS

Frontispiece: Ralph St. Leger and his wife Anne (1468)

1. The Norman invasion, 1066 (Bayeux Tapestry) xvi
2. Principal descendants of Sir Anthony St. Leger 28
3. The Royal Mint, c. 1670 37
4. The original stand at Doncaster 62
5. Park Hill 76
6. Colonel Barry St. Leger; Chief Thayendanega 82
7. Title page from *Tales of Passion* 92
8. First edition of the *Cape Times* 100
9. Title page of *Ballads from Punch* 108
10. Sir Thomas St. Leger and Anne (Plantagenet) 124

ACKNOWLEDGEMENTS

ANYONE WHO UNDERTAKES the task of writing a family history soon discovers he or she is dependent on the full co-operation of many people, relatives, friends and strangers. I have had so much encouragement and help that I could not hope to compile a complete list of all those I should thank. I have to content myself with mentioning a representative few.

Memories of close and distant relatives provided the living link with the past and I am grateful to all those who contacted me to share them. However, two relatives to whom I am especially grateful for their generous loan of family papers which formed the basis of my research are my late grandmother, Gwen St. Leger, and my uncle Antony St. Leger. Without their initial help I could not even have begun. I also wish to thank Eigen Ramsay Murray (née St. Leger) for valuable information about the William Nassau St. Leger line; Rear-Admiral Malcolm St. Leger Searle for his detailed documentation on the South African branch; Julian St. Leger for most useful notes on the Park Hill branch, and for the loan of a photograph; the Chevalier Marc St. Leger for notes on some descendants of the first Viscount Doneraile of the second creation; Beverley St. Leger Hurd for information on some descendants of John Bagot Chester St. Leger; and Jane Godlonton (née St. Leger).

To Roger Longrigg I offer my sincerest thanks for reading the typescript at an early stage and giving me invaluable advice with such kindness.

Thanks are also due to Don Cox; Ruth Morris; Callaghan O'Callaghan; John D. Money; Colonel A. Waller; Dr. and Mrs. Mike Hawker; Vera Ledger; J. M. Pratt; J. L. Markand; Doreen Forsythe; Peter Windows for suggesting the title of the book; Percy Holmes of the Firbeck Local History and N. E. Tomaszewski of the Deal and Walmer History Group, who both shared the fruits of the labours of their groups with me so generously; Gerald Shaw, whose research into the life of Frederick York St. Leger provided me with the basis of my own account; John Stewart; The Hon. Desmond Guinness of the Irish Georgian Society; E. L. C. Mullins of the History of Parliament Trust; and Barbara Brash, who somehow found time in her busy life to proof-read so expertly.

To that remarkable body of British librarians and archivists who give unstintingly of their time and expertise, I should like to say a big thank-you. Three of their number deserve a special mention: E. Talbot-Rice of the National Army Museum; Grace Holmes, the Hon. Archivist of the Aerary, St. George's Chapel, Windsor Castle; and E. J. Chapman, Chief Librarian of the Doncaster Metropolitan Borough Council Library Service, whose co-operation went beyond everything one dares expect from a library service.

I should like to thank the following for permission to reproduce plates in this book: Her Majesty the Queen (Plate 16); the National Portrait Gallery (Plates 4, 5 and 14); the National Gallery of Ireland (Plates 8 and 9); the Comptroller of Her Majesty's Stationery Office for an Ordnance Survey aerial photograph (Crown Copyright Reserved) (Plate 12); Courtauld Institute of Art (Plate 15); Doncaster Newspapers Ltd. (Plate 29); Wedgwood Ltd. (Plate 26); Francis Sinclair (Plate 25); the National Monuments Record (Plate 2); the British Library (Plate 10); Mr. and Mrs. Paul Mellon (Plate 13); Oxford University Press (Plates 19 and 21); Berni Inns Ltd. (Plates 27, 28 and 30); Herr Miebach (Plates 23 and 24); Sammy Hardman (Plate 17); Mrs. Jane Godlonton (Plate 22). The remaining plates are from the author's own collection.

I should like to thank the following for permission to reproduce illustrations in the text: the municipal authorities of Bayeux (no. 1); the Dean and Canons of St. George's Chapel, Windsor (no. 10); the Victoria and Albert Museum (frontispiece); G. P. Dyer, Curator of the Royal Mint Museum (no. 4); the British Library (no. 7); Bell Brothers (no. 5); T. G. Manby of the Doncaster Metropolitan Borough Museums and Arts Service (no. 6); Oxford University Press (no. 8); Marc St. Leger (no. 9).

Finally, my thanks are due to the following for permission to reproduce copyright textual material: Oxford University Press for material from *Some Beginnings* by Gerald Shaw; Juta and Co. for material from *An Editor Looks Back* by G. A. L. Green; *The Cape Times* for extracts from its early editions; Curtis Brown Ltd. for permission to quote an extract from *Bowens Court* by Elizabeth Bowen; Gill and Macmillan Ltd. for material from *Tudor Ireland* by Margaret MacCurtain; and Methuen and Co. Ltd. for material from *A History of Ireland* by Edmund Curtis.

PREFACE

On a visit to my grandparents when I was fourteen, I once asked my grandfather if our surname was French. He looked at me hesitantly for some moments before opening a small cupboard beside his armchair from which he took a slim, blue book. This he opened and unfolded a large sheet of paper stuck to the inside of the cover, spreading it out on the carpet. There before us lay a chart of thirty generations of St. Legers stretching back to 1066 A.D. I was bewildered. It was the first time I had ever seen a genealogical table, and this was my own family! Slowly I began to notice individual names, alongside those of kings, and events and dates I had learnt about at school: the fascination grew as I cast my eyes over nine hundred years of a family. At that moment English history sprang to life for me.

Many years have passed since that revelation, enough time to mull over the desire born then to discover all there was to be known about those people whose name I bore; time to reflect upon the role families played in the making of history. Indeed, much of the history of England is the history of families and their relationships with the Crown. To them fell the task of governing the country, managing the land and patronizing the arts. The laws of the land were formed and an effective judicial system developed partly through their influence. They led in battles at home and abroad, in peacetime setting fashions in life-style, speech and leisure time pursuits. Set in wide parklands, their homes are the most eloquent expressions of civilization and are amongst the finest examples of domestic architecture in the world. England has not been invaded for nearly a thousand years: so many centuries of undisturbed sovereignty nurtures a security which permeates the bones of a people and possibly accounted for the feeling prevailing before the nuclear age that Great Britain was invincible, and would remain so. The atmosphere created by such security allowed the nobility and the gentry to flourish in a milieu of home-grown gentility. Even today the English gentleman is an object of curiosity and respect.

But the days of great families are nearly past. With few exceptions, their social obligations have been taken over by twentieth century institutions and their homes have been converted into hotels, schools and convalescent homes. Yet families do not die with the disappearance of their estates and responsibilities.

Living in England, Wales, Ireland, South Africa and America today are members of an ancient family who are the descendants of the solitary Norman knight at the top of the chart — Sir Robert de Sancto Leodegario. Mention of their surname invariably elicits a remark about the St. Leger Stakes run annually at Doncaster, the world's first classic race, founded by one of their ancestors. Then questions about the family's history follow, evidence indeed that the race keeps alive an interest in the name and family. This book has been written in reply to some of the questions put regularly to St. Legers. It does not pretend to be a complete family history, but is rather a glimpse of past epochs through the experience of one ancient English family with a French name. If it achieves nothing more than to add a small fragment to the vivid mosaic of English history, it has done much. History is, after all, not merely a record of events chiselled into the tablets of time but living experiences which stamp a nation with its character. Though of Norman extraction, the St. Legers bear the hallmark of an essentially English character forged by nine centuries of English experience.

The connection between the family and the Race is of course another reason for this story to be written.

FIRST PART

1. The invading Normans landing their horses, 1066.

CHAPTER ONE

1066 AND SOME OF THAT

WHEN William the Conqueror stumbled from his ship into the chill, autumnal waters of the Pevensey shore, he was supported by the hand of his knight-in-attendance, Sir Robert de St. Leger.

Few details of an eleventh-century knight can be known, yet this fragment of a legend handed down through generations of St. Legers probably survived because it expresses the romantic desire of an ancient family to remember their very own knight in shining armour as the eternal, perfect gentleman. Reared in the age of chivalry he would not, St. Legers quietly reason, have forgotten his manners even when standing knee-deep in alluvial mud. Indeed, Sir Robert's gesture was to become a symbol of the unwavering support given by St. Legers to their monarch at all times: which of them were motivated by loyalty, and which by self-interest, remains an open question.

The society which produced Sir Robert and his kind was at once chivalrous and brutal. After the Norman victory at Hastings — a triumph for muscles not manners – Sir Robert spent some time at Bexley a short distance away. But the Conquest had only just begun though the consequent takeover was achieved in a fairly leisurely fashion. Unhurriedly, Sir Robert eventually found his way to the place he could ultimately call his own.

Living at the manor house in Ulcombe, an early settlement in the north of Kent, was a pagan Dane whom Sir Robert engaged in battle in 1087. The Dane, no match for a mounted knight practised in up-to-date Continental discipline, was easily overcome and ousted from his home. Here Sir Robert fixed his final abode and Ulcombe Manor, held of the Archbishop of Canterbury on condition of service in the King's army, became the family place for six centuries of his descendants.

The Conquest did not halt at England's shore, indeed Henry II sent an army of knights to invade Ireland in 1170, and it is highly probable that one of Sir Robert's great-grandsons settled there as one of Henry's colonists, since a Sir Thomas FitzAnthony St. Leger held office as King's Steward of Leinster in the reigns of King John and Henry III.

Meanwhile in England St. Legers were multiplying satisfactorily and casting firm roots into their adopted land. Sir Robert's great-great-grandson answered the call with other Kentish gentlemen to accompany Richard I to the Holy Land where he battled at the Siege of Acre. For fifteen years he fought in the Holy Wars, only returning to Ulcombe for the last few years of his life. He was buried in Ulcombe's parish church, having earned for himself the title of 'the Crusader'.

The close association of the family with the monarch in these early days naturally involved shouldering the many duties and responsibilities which go hand-in-hand with the privileges of rank. Sir Ralph, the Crusader's son, was impanelled as a member of the jury for the Grand Assize in King John's reign, and later became patron of Ulcombe Church, rebuilt by the Normans on the site of the Saxon one mentioned in Domesday Book. Numerous members of the family were sheriffs and knights of Kent throughout the Middle Ages (see appendices).

Essentially, however, Sir Robert had fathered fighting men. A knight of old was not simply a landowner owing military service to his lord. He underwent a long and arduous training, first serving his liege as a page, when he waited at table, until he was promoted to squire at the age of fourteen. For the next seven years he was expected to accompany his lord everywhere he went, on the hunting grounds and into the field of battle. All the while he was learning from his elders how to represent the notion of chivalry until he too was called upon to share 'the kinship of all true knights'. At twenty-one, if he had proved himself worthy, he would be dubbed a knight by the king or a great lord, receiving his own sword on this occasion.

The end of the thirteenth century, a period of serious strife between England and Scotland, provided an ideal chance for John, Thomas and Ralph St. Leger to win their laurels. Fighting under the standard of Edward I, all three battled sufficiently bravely at Caerlaverock to earn themselves knighthoods for their 'single exploits'.

One duty laid upon the first knights of the shires was to 'parley' with the king at the King's Court — mainly about financial affairs. In the thirteenth century the king was the central figure of any 'parliament.' To his court, the source and centre of government, of law and justice, he summoned whom he pleased. No hard-and-fast rule governed his choice, and summoning knights from the shires proved far more practical then sending out his officers to meet them as had long been the custom. At the Parliament of 1254 Sir Ralph and Sir Hugh St. Leger were present, the first of many of their kinsmen to represent their shires at the regular parliament held at Westminster which had grown from the meetings at the King's Court.

By the close of the fourteenth century St. Legers were sprinkled over the length and breadth of Kent. Marriage settlements, grants and special land transactions steadily increased the family's already considerable possessions. This was an age when death could strike early in a man's life, and it was not unusual for a widow to bring into her second marriage the manors and lands of her first husband. When Juliana Poteyn married Thomas St. Leger of Otterden, Sheriff of Kent in 1397, she enlarged his own respectable estates with the houses and lands she had inherited from her two deceased husbands. A good catch indeed!

The influence of these early St. Legers grew as their lands increased. Once possessed of a manor, a family could hold it for several centuries, like the great manor of Elnothington in Hollingbourne, granted to Arnuld St. Leger in the reign of Edward III. It stayed in the family for two centuries until Elizabeth I came to the throne. A family permanently anchored to one spot guaranteed the stability of mediaeval society.

The feudal system formed a foundation for a complex social and political structure, although by the thirteenth century the older feudal relationships – those between a lord and his tenants – were coming to be less significant than those between men who shared the same occupation or interests. Fellow-workers in crafts or trades, or indeed in government, gravitated towards one another to form distinctive social groups, 'estates' of society with their own special obligations to the whole community.

The proximity of Ulcombe to London kept the family in close contact with the reigning monarch, and while living in Kent, St. Legers became nevertheless ever more involved with the affairs at court. Edward IV 'graciously inclined' towards the fifteenth-century Ralph St. Leger of Ulcombe, Sheriff of Kent in 1468, and appointed him Constable of the magnificent and formidable fortress Leeds Castle, only a stone's throw away from Ulcombe. The King entrusted him with it for life, granting him one of the great parks bordering the castle 'as a further source of emolument'.

Ralph only enjoyed a brief spell in office as he died the following year, yet this first official connection with Leeds Castle was a portent of the future, since his great-grandson Sir Anthony was later on able to call it his home. One of the finest brasses in England lies over Ralph's burial place in Ulcombe Church. His wife Anne, a slim and gracious figure beside him, must have had a wasp-like waist if a brass really gives a faithful representation of a lady's vital statistics.

Close involvement with the Crown was not always an unmitigated blessing as Ralph's brother, Sir Thomas, discovered to his everlasting undoing. Sir Thomas, a man of some ability and even more ambition, contracted the most favourable marriage in the history of the family by wedding Anne, Duchess of Exeter, sister of Edward IV. It was his second marriage. Although it opened the doors of the royal household to him, it was eventually to close the door of his life.

All went well for him in the beginning. When the unscrupulous Edward invaded France with a large army, Sir Thomas together with three other ambassadors (Howard, Morton and Dudley) was sent to negotiate with the French King, Louis XI, before the fighting began. They persuaded Louis not to go to war with Edward, and even to grant generous pensions to the English king and his councillors (including Sir Thomas). This arrangement delighted both sides.

Sir Thomas's fortunes changed when the King died. On his deathbed Edward bequeathed his realm and his boy heir to the protection of his brother, Richard Duke of Gloucester. Intent from the outset on seizing the throne for himself, Richard was assured by the

Bishop of Bath and Wells that the children of the deceased King Edward and his wife, Elizabeth Woodville, were illegitimate, since the King had already been betrothed to Lady Eleanor Butler when he had married Elizabeth, and betrothal had the force of a legal tie.

When this news was disclosed to his council, Richard was urged to claim his rights. Supported by the mighty Duke of Buckingham and other noblemen who backed his claim to the throne, his coronation took place in Westminster Abbey.

Instantly a rebellion led by Edward's in-laws, the Woodvilles, together with Sir Thomas, one of the chief plotters, broke out in the southern and south-western counties. It began as a movement motivated by differing interests, its leaders genuinely dedicated to restoring Edward's heir, Prince Edward, to the throne, albeit some of the followers were men dissatisfied and dispossessed by the redistribution of offices under Richard's regime.

The imprisonment of the young princes (Edward and his brother Richard, Duke of York, in the Tower of London) enraged the rebels, yet real hope existed for their eventual release and a turn in events. Rumours of their brutal murder threw the movement into confusion and the princes' deaths now became immaterial: Richard had to be removed at all costs.

Buckingham turned against Richard to support Henry Tudor's claim to the throne, whereupon he was promptly proclaimed a traitor. But grave mistakes were made, causing the rebellion to collapse. Buckingham was caught and beheaded in Salisbury and the capture of Sir Thomas and two of his confederates followed swiftly.

Though excessively large sums were offered to ransom him, Richard saw no reason to spare the life of his brother-in-law. Sir Thomas was executed at Exeter in 1483 and his body interred in St. George's Chapel, Windsor, alongside that of his wife. No mention is made of his ignominious end on the copper plate fixed to the wall of their chantry, now called the Rutland Chapel. On a shield above his head are the St. Leger arms, possibly the earliest representation of them in England. The Plantagenet arms appear on the shield above Princess Anne's head and the inscription reads:

> Wythin thys Chappell lyethe beryed Anne Duchess of Exetur suster unto the noble kyng Edwarde the forte. And also the body of syr Thomas

Sellynger knyght her husband whych hathe funde wythin thys College a Chauntre wyth too prestys sy'gyng for eu'more. On whose soule god haue mercy The whych Anne duches dyed in the yere of oure lorde M Thowsande CCCClxxv.

Anne, Sir Thomas's daughter by his royal marriage, wed George Manners, eleventh Lord Ros, landlord of an impressive chain of thirty-six manors. They lie buried in the centre of the Rutland Chapel.

Their splendid monument, in a remarkable state of preservation, is not only the finest piece of sculpture in St. George's, but one of the finest of its kind in the country. The Ros tomb is of English alabaster, quite different from the Oriental or Continental kind. Surmounting it are two finely carved recumbent effigies which centuries ago once blazed with vivid colours and gilt. The hands of Lord Ros are bare, on his fingers he wears seven rings; on her tapering, aristocratic fingers, his wife wears only five. The St. Leger Chantry was restyled the Rutland Chapel after their descendants: Thomas, their eldest son, found favour with Henry VIII who created him first Duke of Rutland.

A less splendid yet equally remarkable memorial commemorates Sir Anthony, Sir Thomas's son by his first marriage. The effigy of a knight clad in the armour of the 1530's — though the sculptor has not rendered it with very great accuracy — stands in St. Mary's Church, Slindon, Sussex. It is one of the six remaining *wooden* monumental figures of this period in England, indeed one of the rarest memorials in the country. As a child, Hilaire Belloc was captivated by this unnamed figure lying quietly in a country church and expressed his nine-year-old curiosity and fascination in a poem.

The Nameless Knight

There is no name upon his grave
If his grave it haps to be
And his face doth look towards the plain
And towards the calm blue sea.

He lies in a quiet church aisle
With a small churchyard in view
By a little Gothic window
And 'neath a shadowy yew.

> He may have been carved for ages
> And oft heard the tolling bell
> And he may lie for ages more there
> In that church aisle — who can tell?
>
> There is no name upon his grave
> If his grave it haps to be
> And his face doth look towards the plain
> And towards the calm blue sea.

Little is known of Sir Anthony beyond the fact that he married Elizabeth Digby, daughter of Thomas Digby, 'gentleman of the body to King Henry VII', and settled in Bottesford in Leicestershire not so very far from Bosworth Field. That Sir Anthony took up arms against Richard III with his father, and fought at the Battle of Bosworth to avenge his father's execution seems a distinct possibility.

A fragment of historical evidence suggests his presence at the Court of Henry VIII. The name of Sir Anthony St. Leger occurs on a list of the gentlemen of the Privy Chamber in 1525, and a story lingers on intimating a curious connection between him and the downfall of Cardinal Wolsey. David Lloyd records how he accidentally uncovered a plot against the Crown:

> 'Caesar was the first that came to undo the commonwealth sober; Sir Anthony St. Leger was the first that saved this kingdome, drunk: for in being abroad one night very late, and much distempered, he must needs fancy an extraordinary light in the Cardinal's closet; with which fancy he ran to the king, and although much in drink, prevailed with him so far, that he sends to the Cardinal, and there finds that Juncto that threatened his Kingdome.'

A strange affair recorded nowhere else in official records.

Sir Thomas's youngest brother, James, moved down to Devon to take up residence at Annery, a spacious country mansion which his wife, Anne Butler, co-heiress to Thomas the seventh Earl of Ormonde, had brought into the marriage.

Anne's sister Margaret married Sir William Boleyn, Anne Boleyn's grandfather, a favourable enough marriage at the time. But family ties snapped all of a sudden with the execution of the Butler kinswoman, Anne Boleyn. Her death sowed the seeds of a·century-long feud between the great Butler clan and the St. Legers since Anthony St. Leger of Ulcombe, one of her Kent 'cousins', played a prominent part in her downfall by having sat as a member of the Grand Jury of Kent which found a 'true bill' of indictment against her. The Butlers never quite forgave the St. Legers for their part in putting an end to the numerous favours granted to them while Anne was Queen of England.

In the beautiful Devon countryside the family flourished for several generations, and it was here that Mary St. Leger married Sir Richard Grenville, the celebrated naval hero. In his last fearless stand against the Spaniards off Flores in 1591, he engaged the Spanish fleet with his small ship, the Revenge, until the craft was reduced to a creaking wreck. Lying mortally wounded upon deck, he commanded his master gunner to blow up the ship rather than surrender, but the Spaniards ceased their fire out of respect for a gallant seaman, and their ships drifted silently round the Revenge, flags lowered in tribute as Sir Richard drew his last breath.

Grenville's death was an immeasurable loss to the St. Legers. The intelligence he had so successfully applied to naval tactics had been equally well-employed in family affairs at home and in Ireland, the land which was to shape the future for so many St. Legers.

Not only was Mary left without a husband; for some mysterious reason her family fled from Devon. Mary's father, Sir John, sold Annery to his son-in-law, Tristam Arscott, and got rid of the spoils of the church — lands and property granted by Henry VIII after the dissolution of the monasteries – to his father Sir George, Anne Boleyn's cousin. Sir John's decision to strip the Devon branch of the family of its wealth might well have been motivated by pangs of conscience about having received 'stolen' church property, yet why he should have left one of his sons to live and die in utter poverty remains unexplained.

A generation later not one St. Leger was left in Devon. The timber Tudor mansion was eventually replaced by one of stone, removing all visible trace of the family's existence at Annery where they had 'lived in great port'. A brass commemorates Sir James in Monkleigh Church yet there still endures a more lasting memorial — Sellinger's Round, dedicated by William Byrd to the Devon St. Legers.

CHAPTER TWO

A WISE AND WARIE GENTLEMAN

ONE of the most neglected figures of sixteenth century history must surely be Sir Anthony St. Leger, Knight of the Garter. At the time of his death on the 16th March, 1559, he was so highly esteemed by his countrymen that the public funeral arranged for him was, even by sixteenth-century standards, a glittering and pompous occasion. He was buried with a standard, a great banner of arms, helmet, crest, target and swords, and six dozen escutcheons, in the presence of two heralds, Garter King of Arms and Lancaster Herald.

Anthony, born in 1496, was the first of nine children to be born to Ralph and Isabel of Ulcombe. His education was comprehensive in the most desirable sense:

'When twelve years of age he was sent for his grammar learning with his tutor to France, for his carriage to Italy, for his philosophy to Cambridge, for his law to Grayes-Inne; and for that which completed all the government of himself, to court; where his debonnairness and freedome took with the King, and his solidity and wisdom with the Cardinal.'[1]

At eighteen Anthony, evidently a young man of integrity and intelligence, joined the retinue of George Neville, Lord Abergavenny, an association which grew later on into a family tie. Sir Anthony's son, Sir Warham, married Ursula Neville, one of Lord Abergavenny's daughters, and her sister Catherine married Sir John St. Leger, one of Anthony's Devon nephews. The maidens of the prestigious Neville clan clearly possessed something which the St. Legers appreciated.

Anthony's career initially took shape behind the scenes. He seems to have been considered a most able public servant and was unobtrusively present on many historic occasions; before he was forty, however, he had risen to some prominence at court. Wolsey's protege, Thomas Cromwell, chose him to be his agent in supervising the dissolution of the monasteries when papal power was abolished in England in 1534. Two years later his close friend Sir Thomas Wyatt, then Sheriff of Kent, nominated him as a member of the Grant Jury of Kent which found a 'true bill' against Anne Boleyn.

In being party to the judgement which sent the Queen to the block Anthony sacrificed any working relationship he might have had with his relations the Butlers, whose prestige increased in the sixteenth century as a result of the support they had given Henry Tudor in his fight for the English Crown.

But his friendship with Wyatt, once an intimate friend of Anne Boleyn, remained intact. On Wyatt's death in 1542 Anthony wrote the *Epitaph upon Sir Thomas Wyatt the Elder*[2] which expresses his own personal respect and admiration for the man.

> Wyatt resteth here, that quick could never rest:
> > Whose heavenly gifts increased by disdain;
> > And virtue sank the deeper in his breast:
> > Such profit he of envy could obtain.
> A head, where wisdom mysteries did frame;
> > Whose hammers beat still in that lively brain,
> > As on a stithy*, where some work of fame
> > Was daily wrought, to turn to Britain's gain.
> A visage stern, and mild; where both did grow
> > Vice to contemn; in virtue to rejoice:
> > Amid great storms, whom grace assured so,
> > To live upright, and smile at fortune's choice.
> A hand that taught what might be said in rhyme;
> > That rest Chaucer the glory of his wit.
> > A mark, the which (unperfected for time)
> > Some may approach, but never none shall hit.
> A tongue, that served in foreign realms his King;
> > Whose courteous talk to virtue did inflame
> > Each noble heart; a worthy guide to bring

* forge or anvil

Our English youth, by travail unto fame.
An eye, whose judgment no effect could blind,
　Friends to allure, and foes to reconcile;
　Whose piercing look did represent a mind
　With virtue fraught, reposed, void of guile.
A heart, where dread was never so imprest
　To hide the thought that might the truth advance;
　In neither fortune lost, nor yet represt,
　To swell in wealth, or yield unto mischance.
A valiant corpse, where force and beauty met:
　Happy, alas! too happy, but for foes,
　Lived, and ran the race, that nature set;
　Of manhood's shape, where she the mould did lose.
But to the heavens that simple soul is fled,
　Which left, with such as covet Christ to know,
　Witness of faith, that never shall be dead;
　Sent for our health, but not received so.
Thus for our guilt this jewel have we lost;
The earth his bones, the heavens possess his ghost.

Anthony's service during the dissolution of the monasteries earned him a post in April 1540 as a commissioner for the establishment of the Church of Canterbury. After the dissolution of the priory in 1539, it was necessary to consider which religious houses should be the centres of the bishoprics, and the commission decided the Church of Christ, Canterbury, should remain a cathedral, and continue to be the seat of the diocesan and archdiocesan. Sir Anthony's signature appears on the inventory alongside those of Cranmer, Sir Richard Rich, Sir Christopher Hales, John ap Rees and William Cavendish.

His efforts were richly rewarded by grants of extensive lands and property, including many manors and rectories previously held by St. Augustine's Abbey, which had suffered the same fate as all the other abbeys and priories of England. A further grant was made to him of the Abbot's London House, the ancient Inn of St. Augustine in Southwark.

Not surprisingly Anthony's relatives benefited from his influence. Arthur, his brother, until the dissolution Prior of Leeds Priory near

Ulcombe, was installed in 1542 as one of the first prebendaries of Canterbury, appointed by the foundation charter.

Anthony's connection with the newly established Church of Canterbury was not forged solely by the execution of his duty. Agnes his wife was the niece and heiress of the Archbishop of Canterbury, William Warham, in whose honour they had christened their first son William and their second son Warham. Seven children were born to Anthony and Agnes at Ulcombe, five sons and two daughters.

Ulcombe, situated on a ridge near Maidstone, has somehow miraculously escaped the notice of developers. The place remains a haven of tranquillity scarcely changed by time. Well off the beaten track this 'rather obscure and unfrequented place' overlooks green, undulating Kentish hills, a quiet corner of England bathed in antiquity.

The family home upon the height of Ulcombe provided Anthony with the respite he valued when he was able to withdraw for a while from the affairs at court. It is certain he loved the place yet his calling allowed him little time for his family. On the 31st July, 1537, his career took a new turn, marking the beginning of a public life which would take him far away from his beloved Ulcombe.

Henry VIII appointed 'the King's trusty and well beloved servant' as head of a commission of three officers for 'the ordre and establishment to be taken and made touching the whole state of our lande of Ireland, and all and every of our affaires within the same, both for the reduccion of the said lande to a due civilitie and obedyens, and the advancement of the public weal of the same'.[3]

Sixteenth-century Ireland was a mess. The Norman invasion of 1170 had been the beginning of an eternity of strife between invader and native.

Settled in Ireland as colonists, the Normans adopted the Irish language as their mother tongue as well as Irish customs alien to the English way of life, becoming in time fully identified with Ireland. Successive English monarchs tried to govern through the heads of the great Norman-Irish families who constituted the Irish Parliament, theoretically subject to the English Privy Council.

The king of England was however not Ireland's constitutional monarch but merely entitled 'Lord of Ireland'. A great resentment was shared by the Norman-Irish nobility with the great Irish chieftains for what they all felt to be the intolerable situation being caused by the sustained attempts of the English monarchy to impose its will on Ireland. Finally the Fitzgeralds rebelled and Henry VIII was persuaded by the gravity of the situation to take firm measures to restore order in Ireland.

In the Pale — the districts colonized by the twelfth-century Normans, i.e. Cork, Dublin, Drogheda, Waterford and Wexford — English law had prevailed, but by the sixteenth century the Pale had contracted so much that it only consisted of a small district of about twenty miles around Dublin.

Manors, houses, tenements and lands on the borders of the Pale had been abandoned and stood rotting. It was this fraught situation which Anthony and his fellow commissioners were sent to examine.

They arrived in Dublin in early September and on the 26th set out to inspect the regions adjacent to the Pale. Proceeding systematically through Kilkenny, Tippperary, Waterford, Wexford, Dublin, Meath and Louth, they listened to sorry tales told by juries of inhabitants from each district. The juries were composed of the principal gentry from the shires and the most respected merchants of the cities.

All the evidence, given upon oath, of their numerous grievances, is recorded in what remains of the official records of the inquisitions. The hardships, oppression, injustices and distress suffered by these unfortunate people at the hands of both the Norman-Irish and the neighbouring native Irish made a profound impression on Anthony. The following examples speak for themselves:

> Item: the said Jurye present that ... Nicholas Dernes robbed certen fysher men coming to the market of Kylkenny uppon the ryver.

> Item: the said Jurye do present that my Lorde of Ostrey hath forcybly entered Walter Archers landes ... and hath kepeth the possession thereof, with force contrarye to the Statute.

> Item: the said Jurye present that James Grace in the Kinges highe waye, beside Kylkenny, dyd make assault upon Derby Casshys and Robert Keyley, and hym dyd bete, xvj d in money, nombre of Iryshe, and 2 beoffes felonyously from the

said Robert Keyley dyd stele and bere awaye contrarye to the Kinges peace.

Item: the Jurye present that Richard Sertoll, Phillip Purcelles, Onell, Conhurlle Odoley, my Lorde of Ostreyes servauntes, do in the tyme of Lent take up Otes of every ploughman of the countrey of Kylkenny, not paying money therfor ...

Item: the said Jurye do present that Richard St. Leger in a Kinges highe waye, within the lybertye of Kylkenny did with force and arms make assaulte upon Tegge FitzJohn, of the Iryshe town and hym dyd bete and wounde hym so that he was in greate perylle of death ...

Anthony must have been disheartened on hearing that his own distant Irish cousins were not beyond committing such crimes.

After his tour of inspection and inquisitions Anthony remarked that in his opinion it would be difficult to hold Ireland, 'for onelesse it be peopled with others than be there already, and also certain fortresses there bylded and warded, if it be gotten one daye, it is loste the next'. He saved further discussion of the matter for his return to court.

The commissioners' speedy and discreet accomplishment of their task elicited much admiration. In a letter from Ireland to Thomas Cromwell, Agard observed:

'Trewlye, they have takyn great paynz, and in their bussyness here do usse them verrey dyscretelye, and in espechiall, Mr. St. Leger, whom, by reason of his dyscreschion and indyffrensye towardes everye man, is hylye commendyd here; and ryght well he is worthie.'[5]

Anthony returned to England at the end of March the following year, 1538. In June he was appointed one of the gentlemen of Henry VIII's Privy Chamber and in October that year left for Brussels to procure from Queen Maria of Hungary, regent in the Netherlands for the Hapsburg Charles V, a promise of safe passage through Flanders for Anne of Cleves whom he escorted from Düsseldorf back to England to meet her husband-to-be.

In the meantime, the reports of the Irish inquisitions had been read and assessed, and in July 1540 Anthony was constituted Lord Deputy of Ireland. His appointment put Ireland firmly on the threshhold of a new epoch.

The results of the inquisitions furnished Henry with good reasons for a radical change of policy towards Ireland. His new strategy was three-pronged: to win recognition for his spiritual and temporal sovereignty (Anthony had advised him to take this step 'for the Irish have the foolish opinion that the Bishop of Rome is the King of Ireland'); to conquer the country anew by thoughtfully applied force and good administration; to substitute for the old Irish tribal system of land division the English system of land tenure.

In choosing Anthony to carry out this policy he could be sure the task would be conscientiously undertaken. In his *Chronicle of Ireland*, Richard Stanihurst remarks that Anthony 'was a wise and warie gentleman, a valiant serviter in war, and a good justicer in peace, properlie learned, a good maker in the English, having gravitie so interlaced with pleasantnesse, as with an exceeding good grace he would attain the one without pouting dumpishnesse and exercise the other without loathsome lightnesse'.

Anthony saw Dublin again in early August, 1540. While most of the land was peaceful, the Kavanaghs were causing a disturbance just south of the Pale. The Lord Deputy considered his position carefully before taking action, 'his orders were made but slowly so wary he was; but executed quickly, so resolute he was too'.[6]

He invaded their country, 'burning and destroying the same'. Taken completely by surprise by such unexpected tactics, the Kavanaghs submitted, and Anthony, wishing to demonstrate that the King desired their obedience rather than their property, restored their lands to them immediately on condition they were held by knight's service, and the clan kept the peace in future. By such 'gentle handling' he hoped to win their loyalty.

Four months of bitter fighting and hard bargaining with other clans ensued. By Christmas the O'Mores, the O'Connors and the O'Tooles had entered into treaties whereby they surrendered their lands to Henry and had them re-granted on the same conditions as the Kavanaghs. Anthony spent that Christmas at Carlow Castle mediating between the tribal chiefs of the Kavanaghs and the O'Mores in an attempt to settle their own tribal quarrels and personal differences of opinion. In Lloyd's words, 'Caesar came, saw and overcame. Sir Anthony came, saw and settled.'[7]

New Year's Day, 1541, was spent travelling into Munster to receive the submission of perhaps the mightiest of all leaders, James Fitzjohn Fitzgerald, Earl of Desmond. Both men got on so well that a friendship lasting many years flourished between the two families. A visit to Kilmallock followed of which Anthony remarked in a letter to Henry: 'I think none of your Grace's Deputies cam this way this hundreth yeris before'.[8]

Limerick, the stronghold of the O'Briens, was his last port of call. The meeting with the intractable O'Brien turned out to be a frigid encounter and no satisfactory agreement was reached. But two more chiefs yielded: MacWilliam of Connaught and MacGillpatrick of Ossory.

The moment had come. Assembled in Dublin on the 13th June 1541, the Irish Parliament passed the Act giving Henry VIII his new title:

'That Henry, King of England, and his successors, should be styled Kings of Ireland, with all manner of jurisdiction, power, prerogative and royal authority, ecclesiastical and civil.'[9]

Henry had in fact enjoyed power and prerogative under the former title but the Act clarified his position and stamped it with the official seal. A royal pardon accompanied the Act and on the following Sunday a proclamation in St. Patrick's Cathedral promised freedom to prisoners who had been detained for a variety of offences:

'For as much as the hearts of all godly, natural, reasonable, civil creatures be kindled with life and joy, when they hear of the prosperity, triumph or advancement of their natural, Sovereign Liege Lord; — honourable assembly, ye shall understand, that the triumph shewed here this day is done principally to give thanks to God of his great benefits shewed to our most noble and victorious King Henry VIII, and to declare our own gladness and joy, that his Majesty is now, as he hath always of right been, knowledged by the nobility and commons of this his realm of Ireland, to be King of the same; and his heirs to be named, reputed, and taken for evermore, Kings of Ireland, most worthy under God; and for manifestation partly of the gladness of the nobility here assembled, it is agreed by the King's deputy, and the lords spiritual and temporal, and the commons assembled in this parliament, that all prisoners of what estate, degree and condition, however they be detained for murder, felony, or other offences, which the said Lord Deputy may pardon, (treason, wilful murder, rape and debt only excepted), shall be clearly delivered out of prison, or prisons, then where they, or any of them be detained, and all such prisoners, as so shall be delivered, shall have their pardons, frank and free, requiring the same accordingly; and God save the King's Majesty King Henry VIII, King of England, Ireland and France, defender of the faith, and on earth supreme head of the church of England and Ireland.'[10]

Following the alteration of Henry's title, King Harry's groats were coined, two-penny and penny pieces, with a harp on one side.

Lavish celebrations were laid on to celebrate the passing of the Act. There is even a hint of surprise in a letter from Anthony describing the festivities:

> 'The thing passed so joyously, and so miche to the contentation of every person, the Sonday foloing ther were made in the citie greate festinges in their howses with a goodly sort of gunnes.'[11]

Three great chieftains still held out against Anthony: O'Donnell, O'Brien and O'Neill. By August, though, O'Donnell had given in but O'Neill flatly refused to meet Anthony, putting up the fight of his life when his territory was invaded. After several devastating attacks he was forced to surrender and a meeting was arranged to discuss the terms of his submission.

O'Neill eventually travelled to England to surrender his lands personally to Henry himself, receiving in return the title of Earl of Tyrone. O'Brien, in his turn, received the titles of Earl of Thomond and Baron of Inchiquin for his submission and renunciation of his claim to the lands east of Shannon.

Henry was certainly a little irritated by Anthony's liberal distribution of titles and honours, yet his displeasure was far outweighed by the knowledge that Ireland was well and truly his at last, and indeed a manifestly more peaceful place than it had been in years. Furthermore Irish affairs were in a healthier state than they had been for a very long time. Anthony had, in addition to restoring peace, restored the public revenue to good order by introducing a new tax structure and abolishing many old Irish levies. Not only was Henry benefiting politically; the Irish Parliament could pay its way for the first time.

In the winter of 1541 forty Irish nobles made their solemn submissions to the Lord Deputy, for, as Lloyd points out, 'he was the first Viceroy. King Henry's affection would promote him anywhere, but his own resolution commended him to Ireland'. Kneeling before Anthony as a gesture of loyalty the nobles laid aside their girdles, skeans[12] and caps to swear allegiance to the Crown.

The prorogued Parliament assembled again in February 1542 with Anthony presiding, this time in Limerick. Several important Acts were laws; the most rational and equitable laws were those of England but too rational to be imposed on the brutish Irish; therefore our knight, considering that they could not relish those exact laws, to live or be ruled by them, immediately enacted such as agreed with their capacity, rather than such as were dictated by his ability; his wisdome doing what was most fit and convenient, rather than what was most exact, what they could bear more than what he could do ...'.[13]

Proposals were made to Henry concerning the introduction of measures to facilitate a better administration of the country as a whole and for the reorganization of the regions bordering upon the Pale. A proposal to put the government of the country back into the hands of an Irish nobleman was turned down. But Anthony was well aware that the renewal would be doomed to failure if it was restricted to hollow administrative measures. Three things, he said, would settle a state: 'good godfathers and godmothers performing their vows; good householders with authority in their own families; and good schoolmasters educating the youth'. A full account of his plan was sent to Henry, who expressed his approval by granting Anthony lands in Carlow, Kildare, Wexford, Cork and Dublin.

A permanent Council was established in the province of Munster and greater care was ordered to be taken for the preservation of state documents. Moreover, Irish students were to be admitted for the first time to the Inns of Court.

Anthony reached the peak of his career in 1543 when he received the honour of the Garter for his services in Ireland. Soon afterwards, as a demonstration to Henry that Ireland could be made to contribute something towards the war with France – Henry was besieging Boulogne – an Irish contingent of seven hundred men were sent to England. They mustered in Hyde Park, by all accounts a savage band of warriors, and were shipped to France, there to prove themselves 'most useful' in Henry's campaign.

They ravaged the land, destroying property for thirty miles inland from Boulogne. The French were horrified by these men and their bestial behaviour and inquired of Henry whether he had brought men or devils with him. Henry, most amused, quipped a reply and the French retaliated by treating any Irishman who fell into their hands with indescribable cruelty.

One of the services rendered by the Irish in Boulogne was to procure a bull, tie him to a stake and scorch the beast with faggots forcing him to bellow so loudly that all the cattle within animal earshot were induced to race towards the noise as if it were the middle of the mating season. The Irish captured the best of the beef for the camp's stores; ingenious if cruel.

Every successful man has his enemies and Anthony was no exception. A serious rift developed between him and James the 9th Earl of Ormonde, a man ever watchful for an opportunity to trip up his old rival. Sir Anthony decided upon levying certain additional taxes on Irish subjects to support the government, and the Earl so vehemently opposed the measure that at length he sent a charge of high treason against Anthony to England. The quarrel became so acute that both men were finally summoned to England by the King.

Anthony defended himself against the charges, denying every one of them. He did not stand alone. Supporting his word against Ormonde's were the testimonies of a number of Irish lords, Tyrone, Thomond, Desmond, and the barons of Upper Ossory, O'Connor and O'Carroll of Ely who sent a petition to Henry testifying to Anthony's good conduct and administration and asking that a man like him be sent over should Anthony not return. Henry esteemed both men so highly that the Privy Council took great pains to reconcile them, successfully.

Later, however, it was discovered that the quarrel had arisen from grave misunderstandings which had been engineered by a mutual enemy, John Alen, the Lord Chancellor, who had in fact tried to exploit an initially harmless disagreement to remove two powerful rivals at once. Alen was immediately deprived of his office and clapped into the grim Fleet Prison. Ormonde died soon afterwards in mysterious circumstances, poisoned by a meal served in his London home by his own servants.

Sir Anthony returned to Ireland as Viceroy having been retained by Edward VI (or rather, by Somerset, the Lord Protector) on his accession to the throne. With Henry gone the O'Byrnes took the opportunity created by the new situation to annoy the citizens of Dublin but were speedily subdued. Anthony's brother Robert arrived from England to assist him and received a grant from Edward of:

> 'the custody and command of the castle, honour and manor of Dungarvan in the county of Waterford, to have to his own use all the King's rents, farms, fishing customs, profits and commodities thereof, during pleasure, he keep at all times a convenient number in the castle for the safe custody thereof'.[14]

Sir Anthony invaded Leix and Offaly, defeated O'Connor who had been provoked into rebellion by Lord Justice Sir William Brabazon who was set on exterminating the lords of Leix and Offaly to establish an English colony. Anthony took O'Connor and O'More, also defeated, to England, where they were favourably received.

Sir Edward Bellingham succeeded Sir Anthony as Viceroy in 1548, a mistaken choice, it would seem, since Anthony was re-appointed only twenty-two months later. This third appointment was brief, beginning in August 1550 and ending in grave trouble for Anthony in April 1551, brought about by a religious controversy.

In February 1551, Sir Anthony received an order for the introduction of the English liturgy into Ireland. It ran:

> 'To our trusty and well-beloved Sir Anthony St. Leger, Knight, our chief governor of our Kingdom of Ireland.
> Edward by the Grace of God etc.

> Whereas our gracious father, King Henry Eighth of happy memory, taking into consideration the bondage and heavy yoke that his true and faithful subjects sustained under the jurisdiction of the Bishop of Rome, as also the ignorance the commonalty were in; how several fabulous stories and lying wonders misled our subjects in both our realms of England and Ireland, grasping thereby the means thereof into their hands, also dispensing with the sins of our natives, by their indulgences and pardons, for gain, purposely to cherish all evil vices, as robberies, rebellion, thefts, whoredoms, blasphemy, idolatry etc. He, our gracious father King Henry of happy memory, hereupon dissolved all priories, monasteries, abbies, and other pretended religious houses, as being but

nurseries for vice or luxury, more than for sacred learning: He therefore, that it might more plainly appear to the world, that those orders had kept the light of the gospel from his people, thought it most fit and convenient for the preservation of their souls and bodies, that the Holy Scriptures should be translated, printed and placed in all parish churches within his dominions, for his faithful subjects to increase their khowledge of God, and of our Saviour Jesus Christ. We, therefore, for the general benefit of all well-beloved subjects understandings, whenever assembled or met together, in the said several parish churches, either to pray, or to hear prayers read, that they may the better join therein, in unity, heart, and voice, have caused the liturgy to be translated into our mother tongue of this realm of England, according to the assembly of divines lately met within the same, for that purpose. We therefore will and command, as also authorise you, Sir Anthony St. Leger, Knight, our Viceroy of that Kingdom of Ireland, to give spead notice to all our clergy, as well archbishops, bishops, deans archdeacons, as others our secular parish priests within that our said Kingdom of Ireland, to perfect, execute, and obey this our Royal will and pleasure accordingly.

Given at our mannor of Greenwich, Febr. 6, in the fifth year of our Reign.
E.R.'[15]

Sir Anthony received the orders without enthusiasm: to carry them out would mean backtracking on his own instructions to have the whole of the English Communion Service translated into Latin. After some opposition he finally called together the archbishops, bishops and other clergy for a meeting in Dublin to explain what the King wanted. Having performed his formal duty he closed with these words:

'This order is from our gracious King and from the rest of our brethren, the fathers and clergy of England, who have consulted herein and compared the Holy Scriptures with what they have done; to who I submit, as Jesus did to Caesar in all things just and lawful, making no question why or wherefore, as we own him our true and lawful King.'[16]

The possibility that Anthony harboured secret reservations about the 'why' or 'wherefore' offended George Browne, the zealous Archbishop of Dublin, and he complained to the King about Anthony's Catholic inclinations, accusing him of treason (a customary step at the time, when private disputes arose out of matters of state). Sir Anthony's appointment was promptly cancelled and he was recalled to England.

How Catholic Anthony had remained at heart is difficult to judge.

The active part he played in the dissolution of the monasteries and in the reorganization and establishment of the Church of Canterbury appear to be sufficient evidence for his rejection of the 'old religion'.

Yet how much influence his relative, Archbishop Warham, had over him in religious matters remains obscure. Though one of the greatest humanists of his day and initially a supporter of a break with Rome, William Warham had on his deathbed revoked his part in the decision of the English Synod to recognize Henry as Head of the new Church in England. Certainly Sir Anthony considered the reformers far too zealous, being a moderate man himself, and expressed his disapproval to Browne: 'goe to, goe to, your matters of religion will marre all'.

What is more, he had been present at the trial of Sir Thomas More, and it was to him that More's son-in-law turned for an eye-witness account of the proceedings, partly recorded in his *Life of Sir Thomas More*. Sir Anthony gave his 'credible report' to a man known to have loved and revered More. If William Roper's positive account of Sir Thomas More's courageous bearing and flawless self-defence rests upon the evidence from Sir Anthony (amongst others), the latter's sympathy for More and his cause is implicit.

The Privy Council dealt with Sir Anthony's case in January 1552, just a little while after King Edward had banished Anthony from the Privy Chamber. An entry in his journal for the 26th December records:

'Sir Anthony St. Leger, for matters laid against him by the Bishop of Dublin, was banished from my chamber till he had made answer.'[17]

Anthony must have awaited the decision of the Privy Council with some apprehension, but presumably the Council was persuaded by Anthony's defence of himself against Browne's charges. The King was able to write again in his journal on the 22nd April, 1552:

'Sir Anthony St. Leger, which was accused by the Bishop of Dublin for divers brawling matters, was taken again into the privy chamber and sat among the knights of the Order.'

His acceptance was wholehearted. In May, Henry's gift to him of Leeds Castle in Kent, 'the oldest and most romantic of England's stately homes', was formally granted him by Edward. Leeds Castle amounted to a prodigious gift indeed. For three hundred years it had been used as a principal royal residence known as the 'lady's castle' since eight medieval queens had lived there and loved the place. Anne Boleyn's Great Key was housed there during her period as queen.

Henry made many improvements and frequently entertained princes, ambassadors, cardinals and foreign ministers at Leeds. It was here he received the Hapsburg Emperor Charles V on his visit to England.

When the castle passed out of royal hands into the possession of the St. Leger family, it marked the beginning of three centuries of private ownership, quite long enough for it to be forgotten by the public. Its last owner, Lady Olive Baillie, spent a lifetime restoring the castle to its former splendour and prudently passed her magnificent home back into the 'commonwealth' at her death in 1974. Soon afterwards the public was able to visit the castle described by Lord Conway, the noted castle expert, in the following terms:

> 'Wonderful in manifold glories are the great castle visions of Europe. Windsor from the Thames, Warwick or Ludlow from their river sides, Conway or Carnarvon from the sea, Amboise from the Loire, Aigues Mortes from the lagoons, Carcassonne, Coucy, Falaise and Chateau Gaillard — beautiful as they are and crowned with praise, are not comparable in beauty with Leeds, beheld among the waters on an autumnal evening when the bracken is golden and there is a faint mist among the trees — the loveliest castle, as thus beheld, in the whole world.'[18]

In June 1977 the first diplomatic meeting to be held at the castle since Henry's reception of the German Emperor in the sixteenth century occurred, when the Common Market Foreign Ministers met Roy Jenkins, then Foreign Secretary. Leeds was the venue for more high-level talks in July 1978, when the Foreign Ministers of Israel and Egypt (Muhammed Kamel and Moshe Dayan) met Cyrus Vance, the American Secretary of State. The moated castle had come into its own once more.

Anthony's new base at Leeds may have impressed him, but it never replaced Ulcombe Manor as his favourite home. Leeds, magnificent though it was, stood second in his affections, and he always opted for the comforting, familiar home the family had known for generations.

King Edward died prematurely at sixteen only a year later. The appearance of Sir Anthony's name as one of the witnesses to his will testifies to the breach between them having been healed, and to Anthony's restoration to favour.

Sir Anthony's support of Mary Tudor's claim to the throne might seem opportunistic to anyone who fails to understand the nature of the English Civil Service. Sir Anthony clearly saw himself as a loyal servant of the Crown, first and foremost. At Mary's Coronation he was one of the Knights of the Garter who held the pall over her, and soon after was sworn in as a member of her Privy Council and re-appointed as Viceroy in Ireland.

Queen Mary's efforts to revive the Roman Catholic religion led to a depreciation and soon open disapproval of all services rendered in the past to promote the Reformation. Sir Anthony's fortunes were on the wane, and his enemies at Court moved in to topple him for good. As a pretext for his removal, they suggested he had at one time written verses ridiculing transubstantiation. In his history, Campion notes:

> 'Queen Mary, established in her Crown, committed her government once more to St. Leger, whom sundry noblemen pelted and listed at till they shouldered him quite out of all credit: He, to be accounted forward and pliable to the test of King Edward VI, his reign, rymed against the real Presence for his pastime, and let the papers fall where courtiers might light thereon, who greatly magnified the pith and conveyance of that noble sonnet. But the original of his own handwriting (though contrary to his own judgment) wandering in so many hands, that his adversary caught it, and tripped it in his way, the spot whereof he could never wipe out. Thus was he removed, a discreet gentleman, very studious of the state of Ireland, entach'd, stout enough, without gall.'*[19]

On these grounds, for which there remains no substantial evidence and for other matters, he was again recalled from Ireland. Holinshed recounts:

> 'At Sir Anthony's comming over, great matters were laid to his charge and many heavy adversaries he had which very eagerlie pursued the same against him, wherein he so answered that he was not onlie acqited but also

*resolute without rancour.

gained his discharge for ever to pass over anie more into so unthankfull a land.'[20]

This is the first sign that Anthony was thoroughly weary of Ireland. His troubles were by no means over. Sir William FitzWilliam charged him with falsifying accounts and the Privy Council met to discuss the new accusations. Sir Anthony, laid up at Ulcombe with sciatica, could not attend the meeting, so a letter was addressed to him from the Privy Council and sent to Ulcombe requiring him:

'to signifye with speed . . . what ye myndeth to do herin.'

His death prevented him from replying, settling the matter for all time on the 16th March, 1559. A week later his wife Agnes died.

The state funeral for Sir Anthony had already been arranged, posing a problem for the Heralds' Office. There was no precedent for a person of his rank being buried with his wife. The problem was solved by burying Agnes first on the day before her husband's funeral on the 5th April. Over Sir Anthony's tomb in Ulcombe Church the memorial tablet briefly relates the story of his life.

'Sir Anthony Sentleger Knight of the most honourable order of the garter, gentleman of the privie chamber and employed in the most honourable offices under the most renowned Henry the eight and Edward the sixt Kinges, twice Lord Deputy of Ireland, by whose meanes in his first government the Nobilitie and commons there were induced by generall and free consent to geve unto Henrie the eight King of England in that Province allso Regalia Jura, the title and Scepter of Kinge to him and his Posteritie for ever whose Praedecessors before were intituled only Lordes of Ireland. This grave Councellour after this course of life spent in the Service of thies two rare and redoubted Kinges having endured nevertheless some crosses in the tyme of Queen Mary, and yet living to see the foelicious raigne of our present peerlesse Queen Elizabeth, departed Anno Salutis 1559 Aged about 63 yeares.'

How can we place Sir Anthony in history? Seen from the twentieth century when Ireland finally won her age-old battle for independence, it is tempting to dismiss his life as one spent for a lost cause. Yet the question of the lawfulness of imposing its will upon the Irish did not arise for the English monarchy of the past: that Ireland should be ruled by England was for centuries morally defensible and politically expedient.

Indeed, a stranger to European affairs might be forgiven even today for assuming the two offshore islands constitute one political unit. Insights furnishing men with a willingness to acknowledge the right of others to self-determination only emerge after important historical lessons have been learnt. Sir Anthony was truly a product of his time, giving of his best within the context of a sixteenth-century situation.

That he was a man of outstanding integrity and wisdom is sufficiently documented by the works of commentators and contemporary observers. John Vowel records:

> 'This man ruled and governed verie justlie and uprightlie in a good conscience, and being well acquainted in the course of that land, knew how to meet with the enemies and knew how to staie all magistrates and others in their duties and offices: for which though he deserved well, and ought to be beloved and commended yet the old practises were renewed, and many slanderous informations were made and inveighed against him: which is a fatall destinie, and inevitable to every good governor in that land. For the more pains they take in tillage the worse is their harvest; and the better be their services the greater is the malice and envie against them; being not unlike a fruitful apple-tree, which the more apples he beareth, the more cudgels be hurled at him.'[21]

Sir Anthony is part of Irish history, a subject sorely neglected by British schools at which level it is treated as a peripheral study deserving little more than a cursory glance. A life spent for Ireland has often been a life unheeded, destined for oblivion. Furthermore, men remembered by history are in general the supernovas whose lives are shaped by one burning ambition or passion and who scorch their paths into the chronicles of mankind. Sir Anthony was no such man. He was a person of divers talents, remembered by Lloyd as:

> '... neither souldier nor scholar nor statesman, yet he understood the way how to dispose of all these to his countries service and his master's Honor; being all of them eminently, though none of them pedantickly and formally in himself ... there was none more grave in council in the morning: none more free at table at noon: none more active in the afternoon: none more merry at night.'[22]

Sir Anthony, with his inbuilt sense of justice, embodied that curious marriage of might and modesty that made the English great. Professor Edmund Curtis, the noted twentieth-century Irish historian, generously describes him as 'an Englishman of the old aristocratic type, and a fair-minded man who saw no reason for depriving lords or the Church of their just liberties',[23] and considers that the success of Henry's Irish policy was largely due to Sir Anthony.

The student of Irish history might be inclined to assume that Irish historians would only take a very dim view of an Englishman who initiated a policy which gave England a tighter grip on Ireland. Surprisingly, this is not so. The contemporary Irish historian Margaret MacCurtain claims that 'by 1547 no other Englishman had such an intuitive grasp of Irish affairs and no Englishman of his time was so universally esteemed in Ireland as Anthony St. Leger.'[24] Both views say much for the magnanimity of Irish historians of today.

How then remember Anthony? Terror of the monks? Courteous conqueror of Ireland, holding a sword in one hand and the English Bible in the other? Or simply as an ever-faithful servant of his monarch and country, deserving a title still coveted today: Sir Anthony St. Leger, K.G., Gentleman.

Sir Anthony K.G. = Agnes d. of Sir Hugh Warham.
Lord Deputy of Ireland
nat. 1494 ob. 1559

Children of Sir Anthony:

- **William** — oldest son, disinherited
- **Jane** ob. 1562
- **Anne**
- **Sir Warham** — Sheriff of Kent, Prov. Marshall of Munster ob. 1597
- **Nicholas** 3rd son
- **Robert** 4th son ob. 1564
- **Sir Anthony** 5th son ob. 1613

Line of William:
- **Sir Warham** — Killed by Maguire ob. 1599
- **Sir William** — Lord President of Munster ob. Doneraile 1642
  - **Sir William** — Killed at 2nd Battle of Newbury in Service of Charles I ob. 1644
    - **John** ob. 1696
      - **Arthur, Baron Kilmayden & Viscount Doneraile** ob. 1729
        - **Arthur, 2nd Visct.** ob. 1734
          - **Arthur Mohun, 3rd Visct.** ob. s.p. 1749
          - **Hayes, 4th Visct.** ob. s.p. 1767

    - **Barbara** — married Lt. Col. Heyward St. Leger, 2nd husband ob. 1685

Line of Sir Warham (Sheriff of Kent):
- **Anthony** ob. 1602
- **Sir Warham** — comrade of Raleigh, sold Leeds ob. 1631
  - **Sir Anthony** — Warden of the Mint, sold Ulcombe ob. 1680
    - Dukes of Leeds and Rutland.
  - **Lt. Col. Heyward** — 2. s. & h. Heyward's Hill, Co. Cork, married Barbara d. of Sir William Lord President of Munster ob. 1684
    - **Warham** s. & h. Heyward's Hill.
      - **Elizabeth** — married Richard Aldworth, Freeman, inherited Doneraile Court ob. 1773
        - **St. Leger Aldworth** (2nd son) — assumed name of St. Leger, created Baron & Viscount Doneraile (2nd creation) ob. 1787

Viscounts Doneraile
2nd	Hayes	ob. 1819
3rd	Hayes	ob. 1854
4th	Hayes	nat. 1818
5th	Richard	nat. 1825
6th	Edward	nat. 1866 ob. 1941
7th	Hugh	nat. 1869 ob. 1956
8th	Richard	nat. 1923 title not confirmed.

Table showing principle descendants of Sir Anthony St. Leger K.G.

2. The principal descendants of Sir Anthony St. Leger, K.G.

CHAPTER THREE

THE LEGACY

SIR ANTHONY'S second son, Sir Warham, inherited the Castle of Leeds, the Manor of Ulcombe and the perplexing problems of Ireland. His elder brother, William, was not mentioned in the will for some undisclosed reason, possibly because he had already been catered for in Ireland.

Sir Warham spent his youth in England; it was hardly the carefree time his father had enjoyed as a young man at Court. He accompanied Somerset in his invasion of Scotland in 1547 when he was barely twenty-two, was captured and held prisoner for two years until ransomed for one hundred pounds.

A few years later circumstances forced him to take up arms against Sir Thomas Wyatt the Younger when he led the men of Kent in rebellion on London in protest against the ascent of Mary Tudor to the throne which they believed belonged rightfully to Lady Jane Grey. During the reign of Queen Mary, Sir Warham may have served for a time under his father in Ireland. In 1560, he held office as Sheriff of Kent but not for long. The son of a man so well versed in Irish affairs seemed ideally suited for an Irish destiny too: his election to the Irish Privy Council and his knighthood in 1565 could have surprised no-one.

Queen Elizabeth decided to establish a government in Munster with its own president. Since it was one of the provinces of the English Pale won back for the Crown by Sir Anthony's efforts, it seemed natural that Sir Warham should receive the job and he was duly nominated by the Viceroy, Sir Henry Sidney, who had turned his attention to the anglicizing of Munster.

Sir Warham, expecting to obtain the post, worked at his duties from January 1566 until November 1568. Queen Elizabeth, however, refused to confirm the post, conceivably acting on the advice of her great favourite and Butler kinsman, Thomas, tenth Earl of Ormonde, whom she had appointed general of the royal forces in Munster. As her pretext she objected to Sir Warham's friendliness towards the Earl of Desmond, whose clan, the Fitzgeralds – arch-enemies of the Butlers – had a long history of rebellion. Elizabeth understandably favoured Ormonde for the post, though finally Sir John Perrott was chosen, taking up his duties a good while later.

Early in 1565 Sir Warham had been ordered by the Queen to arrest the Earl of Desmond for quarrelling with Ormonde, who was summoned to London to give an explanation. Sir Warham's reluctance to carry out the order irritated Her Majesty, but he finally obeyed. She was nevertheless very annoyed: Sir Warham was recalled from Ireland and returned to Leeds Castle. His break from Irish affairs, however, was to be short-lived.

The Earl of Desmond and his brother Sir John were imprisoned in the Tower of London and on their release in 1570 Sir Warham was given custody of them and their families, about thirteen people. He decided to hold them in the old house at Southwark, renamed Sentleger House after it had been granted to Sir Anthony at the dissolution.

Once known as the Inn of St. Augustine when owned by the Abbots of St Augustine's, Canterbury, it had probably become the London residence of Sir Anthony. The rambling stone and timber-built house, with its many rooms, wide passages and staircases, and numerous galleries, provided a spacious enough setting for the thirteen 'prisoners'.

Sir Warham had been encumbered with an onerous task. For the next two years, the Earl and company lived with him, for most of the time at his own expense. Sir Warham's repeated requests to the Privy Council went unheeded for a long time. In a letter dated 17th October, 1570, addressed to the Privy Council, Sir Warham writes:

'My dutie don to your Honors, having writen a letter unto your Honors a ten weekes since, for th'understanding of your pleasure howe I should be answered for th'erle of Desmond's dyet, his lady and his brother Sir John of Desmond, and their famellies; as also for th'understanding of your

further pleasure what libertie they should have, having had one at the Courte ever since attending for your Honor's answeares; These may be most humbly to beseech your Honors that I may have a warrant for receipt of money for their diets; otherwise I shall be constreyned to bring them to ye Court, being not able, by my great losses susteyned in Ireland, to beare the charges thereof any longer, they being to the nomber of thirteene or fourteene persons, not having anything of their owne to reliefe themselves with all, — saving your Honors, not so much as to buy them a peir of shooes, nor have not had since their comyng into my charge, and stand in despair to have anything out of their own countrie. So, bolde to trouble Your Honors with their causes, so most humbly take my leave from my pooer house of Leeds Castell this 17 of October, 1570.
Your Honors to commaunde,
Wareham Sentleger'.[1]

Indeed, Sir Warham was not only beset with financial problems by his unwelcome 'guests'; he also found he had insufficient control over the headstrong Earl and his brother. In another letter sent from Sentleger House, dated 12th July, 1571,[2] Sir Warham expresses his frustration at the situation, and desires to be discharged of the Earl, or else that he and his troublesome brother should be prisoners in a real sense. A month later the Privy Council received a further letter from him, complaining:

'... that the Earl of Desmond refused to come down into Kent with me ... after my departure out of London, being the eight of this month, the which Earl hath rashly ranged abroad into sundry parts of London ...'[3]

Nights on the tiles? Sir Warham had had enough. Once again he asked to be discharged of his task or to be commanded to 'keep them prisoners without liberty'.

Not surprisingly by August 1572 Sir Warham had reached the end of his tether and refused to enter into any further bonds for the Earl and his brother. Miraculously his firm stand resulted in the Earl and his brother being returned to Ireland. Sir Warham eventually received reimbursement from the Privy Council, albeit only a fraction of what he had spent!

Back in Ireland, the Desmonds rebelled anew and in 1579 the Earl was proclaimed a traitor. Sir John died rebelling in 1581, his brother's death following two years later; none could deny their spirit and courage. The Earl's estates were all forfeited, six thousand acres went to Sir Warham while more than twenty thousand were granted to Sir Walter Raleigh. Edmund Spenser received three thousand and twenty eight acres.

Sir Warham, jobless, made repeated petitions for employment. At last his persistence won him the appointment of Provost Marshal of Munster, a predominantly military job. One of his closest allies, Sir Walter Raleigh, speaks highly of him in a letter to Lord Leicester:

> '. . . I will not trouble your Honor with the business of this lost land, for that Sir Warram Sentleger can best of any man deliver unto your Lordship the good, the bad, the mischiefe, the means to amend, and all in all of the common wealth, or rather the common woe. He hopeth to find your Honor his assured good Lord, and your Honor may most assuredly command him. He is loveingly inclined towards your Honor, and your Lordship shall win by your favour towards him a wise, faithful and valiant gentleman, whose words and deeds your Honor shall ever find to be one. Thus having no matters, but only I desire continuance of your Honor's favour, I shall take my leave. From camp at Leismore, in Ireland, August 25 1581.
>
> Your Honor's faithful and obedient
W. Rauley.[4]
>
> To the Earl of Leicester.'

The death of the Desmond chiefs left the way open for Elizabethan colonists to settle in Munster, cultivate the land and impose English law and 'civilitie' in the Province, thereby reducing the danger of the Spaniards using Ireland for an attack on England. The acute fear of a surprise Spanish invasion kept Elizabethans constantly alert and vigilant. Spies were everywhere and rumours of the impending invasion rife. The Queen was kept well informed. In a letter to her, Thomas, Earl of Ormonde writes in 1583:

> 'Since the dispatch of my last advertisements to your most excellent Majesty, I found here at Limerick one Bartholomew Whyte, a merchant . . . come from Spain, who being examined told me that he had conference with a countryman of his that waits on James Fitzmorris . . . who told him for troth, that presently upon the return of James Eustace from Rome . . . the King of Spain determined to send hither with him some part of his army lately come from the Ferseros, the same news also he said were confirmed to him by the oath of a traitor, Prest, fled from this land into Spain

The Legacy

which in discharge of my duty, I have thought fit to certify to your highness . . .'

Ormonde, the old St. Leger enemy, does not waste this opportunity to throw new suspicion on Sir Warham. He continues . . .

> 'I may not omit in respect of the same to let your Majesty understand that by examining some of the traitors it is declared that Sir Warham St. Leger did send advice to the traitor Desmond (longe afore he was slain) to stand out and not submit him to me saying I should have been shortly removed and upon the coming of another governor he should be received to your highness' mercy.'[5]

Sir Warham retaliated by accusing Ormonde, by then the Governor of Munster, of high treason, and at the same time laid before the Queen proposals for the better government of Ireland.

The thankless task of fighting Irish rebels occupied the rest of Sir Warham's life, leaving him all too few opportunities to return to England. For a brief period in 1594 he stayed at his romantic castle home but soon had to return to Ireland to govern Munster himself.

He was probably instrumental in the choice of Anthony, his youngest brother, for the post of Master of the Rolls in Ireland, a newly created job under Elizabeth. Sir Warham died in Cork in 1597, having given half his life and all his energy for the Crown in Ireland.

* * * * *

A curious feature of St. Leger history is the phenomenally high number of second marriages, so many in fact that one might be forgiven for suspecting that a St. Leger did not really consider himself properly wed until he had indulged in the sport twice over. Sir Warham had been no exception. His wife Ursula, daughter of George Neville, Lord Abergavenny, produced nine children and with a sigh expired.

A closer look at Sir Warham's family reveals the kind of tragedy which stalked all large families of the sixteenth century when infant mortality was as common as flu today. Sir Warham lived to the grand old age of seventy-two years, yet his oldest son, Sir Anthony, heir to Ulcombe and Leeds, obviously did not inherit his father's longevity, dying only five years after him in 1602. Only Sir Anthony's brother George outlived him. Nicholas, Henry and William, the other boys in the family, were all laid to rest before they reached manhood. The two girls to survive were Anne the oldest and Jane the youngest, poignantly christened after a baby which had died shortly before Jane's birth. Another sister, Mary, died in girlhood.

Anne married Thomas Digges, Master General of the Low Countries, and, defying all the pernicious threats to health which were ranged against even the toughest constitution, enjoyed an astonishing lifespan of eighty-one years.

But who was to inherit Sir Warham's Irish lands and houses? The land of the landed gentry guaranteed the economic survival of a family and ultimately the stability of society. It was all worthless without an heir. Emeline Goldwell, Sir Warham's second wife, produced the solution: Walter. He inherited all his father's possessions in Cork and Carrickline.

* * * * *

Anthony's eldest son was christened Warham after his grandfather and knighted in 1608. It is from his marriage to Mary, daughter of Sir Rowland Heyward, twice Lord Mayor of London, that the majority of St. Legers living today are descended. Sir Warham II was also closely associated with Sir Walter Raleigh[6] who generously described him as 'an exceeding valiant and worthy gentleman'. Sadly, it was a friendship which was to end in calamity.

Sir Warham II was induced to give considerable financial support to Raleigh's ill-fated expedition to Guiana in search of Eldorado. The fleet which set sail from Cork Harbour consisted of the Admiral's ship and thirteen others.

The first ship was the Destiny of 440 tons, 36 pieces of ordnance and 200 men. Sir Walter Raleigh took command and his son was the captain. The second ship was commanded by Captain John Pennington and the third, the Thunder, by Sir Warham II. It was 150 tons 20 pieces of ordnance, 6 gentlemen, 60 soldiers and 10 landsmen.[7]

At Cliana, Sir Warham II and Sir Walter fell ill. Raleigh ordered

The Legacy

Keymiss, a Captain of the Fleet, to sail into Oronoko with five small ships to discover a mine. Keymiss failed to find it and the Fleet dispersed having achieved nothing.

On his return to England empty-handed Raleigh was executed to appease the Spaniards and Sir Warham, financially ruined, was forced to sell Leeds Castle to a relative, Sir Richard Smith, son of 'Customer Smith' who made his fortune by pocketing the proceeds of the customs of Queen Elizabeth.

Leeds did not stay long in Sir Richard's possession, being sold to yet another relative, Sir Thomas Culpepper, Sir Warham's son-in-law. Strenuous efforts were made to keep the place in the family but it was not to be, and the 'beautiful palace in Kent' (Froissart 1394) passed out of their possession for ever.

Ulcombe Manor stayed in the family for another thirty years when it too was sold by Sir Warham II's oldest son, Sir Anthony.

Sir Anthony's decision to part with the family home may well have been precipitated by his enforced absence from Kent. His appointment as Warden of the Royal Mint which he held for three periods amounting to thirty-four years required his undivided attention in London. At the Mint, housed in the Tower of London at that period, a house and a garden beside the Jewel Tower went along with the job.

The Warden seems to have acted mainly as the custodian of the prerogatives of the Crown in all matters related to coining. His duties involved checking the Master of the Mint and his workers, collecting the dues of the Mint and accounting for its expenditure, and seeking out counterfeiters. In addition to the usual administrative duties, he was responsible for the design of new coins.

Sir Anthony's periods of office lay within the reigns of Charles I and Charles II. At the beginning of his reign, King Charles II addressed an order to Sir Anthony and Sir William Parkhurst, co-warden, authorizing them 'to make, or cause to be made, all sorts of irons etc. for the well making and imprinting of the new Monies'.[8] These 'new Monies' were to replace the hammered coins of Charles I's reign. The wardens were to set an engraver to work 'to draw and grave all such patterns and irons with the King's effigies, title etc. according to such directions and commands as they should receive from His Majesty'.[9]

During Sir Anthony's second period of office a new Act was passed by Parliament which among other changes released the Warden from certain duties which were in future to be discharged by the Master. The Warden, while retaining his position as principal of the Mint and making himself a nuisance now and again as a reminder to the officers of his continued presence there, ceased to take much part in the day-to-day running of the Mint. Thomas Fowle, the comptroller's clerk, remarks in 1696:

> 'Since his coming to the Mint, which was about the 20th July 1672, Sir Anthony St. Leger, then Warden of the Mint, came very seldom to the place and did not anything of service more than come and ask how the affairs of the Mint were, and that was all, and so went away.'[10]

Indeed, a most leisurely way of earning four hundred pounds per annum.

Of Sir Anthony's fourteen brothers and sisters, seven died in childhood: conquering death by numbers was still the only way of ensuring the survival of a family. The notion of the unwanted child had not been conceived; every child was desperately necessary — in case it should live.

Only Anthony's sister, Ursula, remained in Ulcombe as the wife of the rector, Daniel Horsmanden. His brothers, Rowland and Heyward, settled in Ireland, Rowland as Governor of Bandon in Cork.

Yet another brother, Dudley, moved with Anne, his Ulcombe-born wife, farther north to Thanet and his descendants settled in the area. Their son, also Dudley, held office as Lieutenant of Deal Castle in the second half of the 17th century, an important period for the town of Deal. In 1698 the people decided it was time Deal pressed for a Charter to make the port a Corporate and Market town. Dudley appears as one of the twenty gentlemen elected as managers 'to carry forward and obtain a grant of such a charter'.[11]

Edward his son, having no military aspirations, became a surgeon and returned to practise in his home town. He was one of the proprietors of a private hospital at a time when the port is described in State Papers as one of the four greatest ports of England, alongside Rochester (where Sir Thomas had been Lieutenant in his time), Portsmouth and Plymouth.

Marlborough, engaged in the early battles of the War of the Spanish

The Legacy

Succession being fought on the other side of the Channel in the Netherlands, depended on the fleets assembled in the Downs to ship the army across. It was left to the people of Deal to keep the fleets well stocked with provisions and to care for the sick being landed at the port in large numbers. Dr. Edward St. Leger had contracted for the care of the injured but came up against a problem which sounds all too familiar: he discovered the government was a bad paymaster. In 1705 he could not obtain his fees. The situation worsened when his colleagues also failed to squeeze a single sovereign from the government, and since then as now a hospital cannot be run on devotion and patriotism alone, it had to close down six years later. However, it was reopened and continued to be maintained privately until the end of the eighteenth century.

This east Kent line lasted one generation more, leaving only one or two St. Legers in the county. The first flowering of a family had already drawn to a close. With the passing of the Tudors the rose began to wither. What remained of the legacy fermented in Ireland where the family was casting new roots.

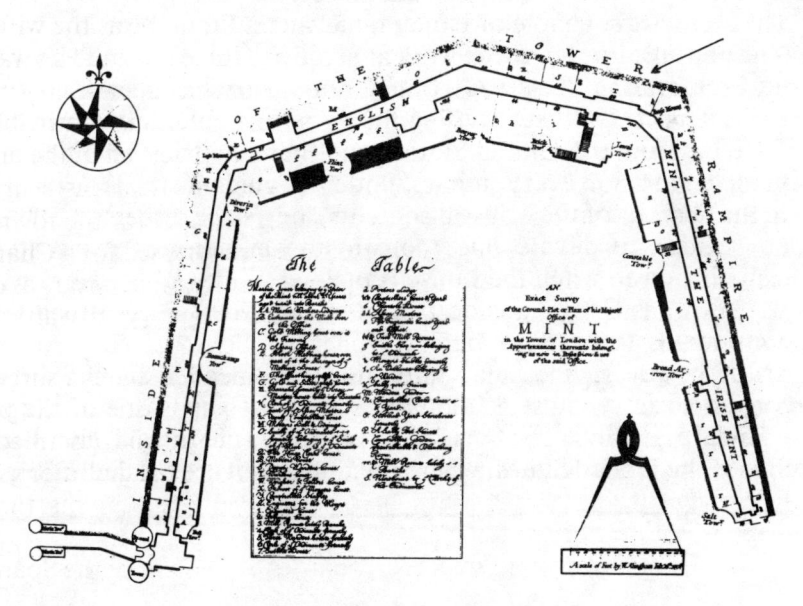

3. The Tower of London, where the Royal Mint was housed in 1670. Sir Anthony's house marked by an arrow.

DONERAILE COURT

A note on its history and restoration by the Irish Georgian Society

In 1969 Doneraile Court was acquired by the Department of Lands so that its park of 600 acres could be made into a wildlife preserve as an amenity for the people of Cork. This has been done extremely well; the park, with its quarter-mile of formal fishponds and its four different herds of deer, was opened to the public in 1984. The house, already in poor condition, was abandoned and suffered from vandalism. In 1976 the Department presented a lease of the Court to the Irish Georgian Society, who began the lengthy and arduous task of rescuing it from decay. The principal contributor to the cost of the work has been the Samuel H. Kress Foundation of New York, via the International Fund for Monuments. Support has also been received from Bord Failte and the Cork County Council, and many benefits have been arranged in the vicinity by Edmund Corrigan, the Cork representative of the Irish Georgian Society.

The architect in charge of Doneraile Court is Frank Murphy, who was responsible for the rescue work at Skiddy's Home in Cork, for the Cork Preservation Society. Arthur Montgomery has been living in the Court since 1969, supervising the work in a voluntary capacity. Volunteers from the United States and other countries have helped with the restoration every summer under his guidance.

In the absence of the original contents, long since dispersed, it has been decided to devote one room to the memory of the writer Elizabeth Bowen when the house is opened to the public. Her own house, Bowens Court, was destroyed in the 1960s. A great deal of work remains to be done before Doneraile Court is ready to be opened, however, and funds are still badly needed by the Irish Georgian Society, whose headquarters are at Leixlip Castle, Leixlip, Co. Kildare, Ireland. The Society is a registered charity in Ireland, as well as in the United States, where donations to it are tax deductible.

CHAPTER FOUR

DONERAILE

DONERAILE is an ageless place whose history contains all the chief elements in the vivid saga of Ireland. Yet, few have ever heard of this compact little town wedged in a fold of the quiet Cork countryside, and fewer still are aware that it was once a sufficiently important spot to merit larger lettering than Mallow on ancient maps.

Anyone coming along the old Mallow Road for the first time in search of Doneraile, finds himself slowing down instinctively when the place comes into view. There, spread gracefully across a hillside descending to the town of colourwashed cottages, lies Doneraile Park, deceptively imitating a carefully landscaped garden. It is part of the old demesne surrounding Doneraile Court, the mansion built by 18th-century St. Legers upon a vast, idyllic estate stretching over lands familiar to the family since Elizabethan times.

Doneraile rises gradually from the banks of the River Awbeg, the 'gentle Mulla' of Spenser's *Fairie Queene*. Its waters follow an unchanging, meandering course through the sylvan scenery of the old demesne. Little remains in Doneraile now to serve as a reminder of past turbulence and bloodshed.

Once upon a time, *Don* or *Dún ar Aill** was an ancient 'fort on a cliffe'; later a castle was built there by the powerful local Synan family, who held it with several other castles in the district until the sixteenth century.

---

*Doneraile

The association of the St. Legers with the place began in 1639 when the castle was occupied by Sir William St. Leger, great-grandson of 'the wise and warie gentleman'. Sir William's father, Sir Warham III (son of the disinherited William) had spent his entire life in Ireland for the cause of the Crown. Initially employed in the government and defence of Leix and Offaly, he was eventually elected to the Irish Privy Council and became governor of Leix and a commissioner for the government of Munster. A serious leg injury received in a battle with rebels made him lame in later life, but not before he had earned himself a reputation for valour amongst his English contemporaries.

His death came about violently. About a mile from the gates of Cork City he engaged Hugh Maguire, Lord of Fermanagh, in a duel in which Maguire was slain. Sir Warham died the same day from his wounds; Maguire had thrust a lance through his skull.

William, his son, had no real choice of career; he followed in his father's footsteps and became a soldier as was expected of him. Evidence suggests he killed someone when he was a young man and had to flee the country. His flight took him to the Continent where he spent about eight years serving in the army in the Netherlands where he met and married a Dutch girl, Gertrude de Vries van Dort, who bore him two children. At long last his exile came to an end when he received a royal pardon from King James I and he was free to return to his native Ireland with his family. Gertrude and their children were speedily naturalized by Act of Parliament in 1624.

As a young soldier Sir William exhibited extraordinary military talent. There was unceasing fighting in Ireland and his service was rewarded by large grants of Crown lands in Queen's County and Limerick. In 1627 he was appointed Lord President of Munster and like his father before him, a Privy Councillor; he also commanded a company of Foot and a troop of Horse.

While described as a 'very noble and just man' and 'a brave and prudent gentleman' he seems to have been a very strict disciplinarian. An order published by him in 1630 commanding steps to be taken against the 'excessive multitude of Irish beggars encumbering England' suggests a harshness which the Irish can hardly have interpreted as noble or just. Constables were charged to whip vagrants and hand them on to the next parish, until they came to some settled course of life. Ships' masters who took them on board were to be imprisoned. A dedicated military man, Sir William evidently had no patience with scavengers and scoundrels; the root of the problem was ignored.

During Wentworth's term as Viceroy, Sir William supported him in his arbitrary measures for maintaining an army, and trained the eight thousand Foot and one thousand Horse raised by Wentworth for his planned invasion of Scotland to quell the Scottish Presbyterians who had risen in rebellion against the attempts of King Charles I to impose his own ideas of doctrine and church government upon them. As Sergeant-Major General of the army in 1640, Sir William was in command of Carrickfergus Castle, one of the largest and best preserved forts in Ireland today.

During his service, Sir William had become a landowner of some standing, having purchased a major part of the lands belonging to the Manor of Kilcolman from Sylvanus, a son of Edmund Spenser, and from Sir Walter Welmond. The purchase was confirmed by the Crown, and Doneraile was created a manor in which Sir William was entitled to hold Court Baron. Yet another purchase from the Synan family extending the demesne was likewise confirmed and re-granted by Charles I. The lands listed by the grant are considerable:

> 'All ye Towns, Villages, Hamlets, Lands and Tenements of Downerayle, Ardgillybert, Ballyredmond, Kilconyllie, Killeronittie, Ballymorne, Sheaglie, Ballyellis, Ardadam, Ballyandree, Kilbracke, Carkerbegg, Bibblockestowne, Castlepook, Craignetrohan, Knockshrughane, Killpatricke, and the moiety of Croghincree.'[1]

Through the grants, Doneraile and the country for miles around became St. Leger property and remained in the family for some three hundred years.

But the sixteen-forties in Ireland were years crowded with confusion. Dark clouds were gathering over Parliament and the English Crown. Irish leaders, living in the woods and mountains of Ulster, waiting for a chance to recover their lost lands, saw them as a favourable omen signalling the time to strike.

They acted. The Great Rebellion of 1641 flared up in Ulster but swiftly engulfed the whole of Ireland, entangling Sir William in a web of soul-sapping circumstances which were ultimately to destroy him. A loyal and fervent Royalist, he was at Doneraile Castle when the rebellion broke out. Such a movement horrified a man who had inherited an age-old fidelity to the monarchy. Vehemently Sir William threw himself into the task of suppressing the rebels, executing without mercy any who fell into his hands.

As the President of Munster he had leave to impose martial law under which many innocent labourers and husbandmen suffered; others were driven to despair and so 'the evil increased'. His uncompromising attitude towards the enemies of the Crown and those in his own ranks 'romishly affected' did not dissuade a contemporary from describing him as a 'brave, gallant and honest man', though he does add the reservation 'but somewhat too rough and fiery in his temper'. A telling anecdote of his brand of gallantry survives.

In the midst of winter, his army was lying at Kildorrey waiting for the Irish forces under Lord Montgarret to attack. A young officer saw Sir William lying on the ground just covered by a heavy snowfall. The whole force, in a state of extreme fatigue and suffering from exposure, encamped without tents or any kind of shelter, was near the end of its strength. The officer offered Sir William his cloak to cover himself but the old soldier, already in the grip of illness, declined, explaining to the young man that he stood more in need of it than himself being less accustomed to the hardships of army life.

His heart ached when he saw men he had trusted defecting; Elizabeth Bowen relates an incident from the outbreak of the rising.

'Lord Cork, still non-committal (as to whether to join the Royalist cause) saw to it that Sir William St. Leger at Doneraile was notified. Sir William was Lord President of Munster, it was for him to act, and if necessary, take the blame.

The next thing that Sir St. Leger heard was that Lord Muskerry was up in arms, at the head of some thousands of Irish rebels. To Sir William, a passionate, faithful Royalist, this looked like one more blow to the King. He raised a force, marched and confronted Lord Muskerry at Redchair, a pass in the Ballyhouras near Killdorrery and drew up for battle.

Lord Muskerry, however, sounded a trumpet, sent out and offered to show St. Leger the King's commission. The King's commission produced and closely examined, reversed for St. Leger the entire matter. His own position now looked ambiguous. To the three Boyles in his party — the Lords Dungarvan, Broghill and Kilmeaky, he said "I would rather die than be a rebel". He disbanded his forces and rode home, though still in trouble of mind.'[2]

Doubts about Lord Muskerry[3] lingered on to be confirmed in April, 1642, when Muskerry led a confederate[4] attack on Cork and invested the city where Sir William lay sick with fever and fraught with distress at the ambiguities of his position. Too weak to command, he delegated authority to his son-in-law, Lord Inchiquin, who drove Muskerry's Irish from the city.

Shortly before his death at Doneraile in 1642, Sir William confided in a letter to James Butler, 12th Earl of Ormonde, Commander of the Royal forces, about his suffering:

> 'It grieves me beyond any earthly sorrow for the great distance and difference betwixt His Majesty and the parliament; and if all the measures of the times, joined by my long and violent sickness, were not of force to subject me to the grave, yet the sorrow for these unhappy variances would crack a much stronger heart, than your servant hath now left in him.'

Sir William's heart finally cracked in July, 1642.

Worse was in store for Ireland. During the English parliamentary troubles of the 1640s there were still men in Ireland who, like Sir William, were willing to lay down their lives for the Crown. Among those who died fighting against Cromwell's troops at the Second Battle of Newbury was Sir William's eldest son and heir, also named William. Cromwell marched into Ireland and scarred Irish racial memory for all time with the atrocities of Drogheda and Wexford when all the inhabitants, men, women, children and babes in arms were butchered without mercy.

Three years after Sir William died, Doneraile Castle fell to the Irish under Lord Castlehaven. Sir Percy Smythe commented:

> 'All our castles and holds beyond Blackwater, Ballhooly excepted, are gone, most burnt to the ground, in particular Mitchelstown and Doneraile.'

The Castle was eventually repaired but lay in ruins once more in 1750. Over its remains, a barrack was erected for a troop of Horse though nothing can be seen today. Sir William had a fine house and a magnificent park near the Castle; it too was burnt down by the Irish, at least one tragedy Sir William was spared the knowledge of.

* * * * *

For his second wife Sir William prudently selected a local heiress, Gertrude Heyward, mistress of a large estate in Rathcooney near Cork City on which stood a spacious mansion. Their daughter Barbara came into the property and settled there with her husband, Lt. Col. Heyward St. Leger, a second cousin whose father had sailed to Guiana with Raleigh. Thus Barbara's marriage did not even involve her in a change of name. Their house became known as Heywards Hill House and for two hundred years was occupied by the family. All that now remains of the mansion at Rathcooney is one gable wall.

Their grandson, Andrew, and his wife Jane were victims of one of the most atrocious murders in the 18th century. One dark November night in 1730, Andrew's manservant, Tim Croneen, saw his master to bed for the last time. Having completed his usual duties around the house, he retired himself to the room he shared with the gardener.

That night he stayed awake and at two o'clock the next morning, crept down to his master's bedchamber and shot him through the head while he slept. Then he pinned the terrified Jane down to the bed, cut her through the nose and stabbed her about eleven times in the stomach. She did not die until seven o'clock, five agonizing hours later. The gardener had been a witness to Croneen's absence from their bedroom so he too was clubbed on the head with a hatchet and stabbed to death.

The news of the slaughter stunned the local gentry. Prompt action was taken to bring the culprit to justice and a reward of 25 guineas offered for the capture of Croneen. The Viceroy followed this up by offering a further one hundred pounds.

Croneen did not get very far and was apprehended shortly afterwards on board a ship bound for France. With him was his accomplice, the servant maid Joan Condon. They were both tried by a special commission set up by the Viceroy and found guilty.

Croneen was executed in January, 1731. The penalty under Common Law for women committing Petty Treason was savage. Joan Condon's sentence condemned her to be burnt at the stake. In practice the victim was strangled before the faggots were lighted, a fate meted out to Miss Condon.

Public opinion held they had both received their just deserts.

* * * * *

The house which became the permanent seat of the St. Legers in Ireland was designed by Rothery and has been described as one of the finest examples of Georgian architecture in that country. It is in fact an architectural mongrel and probably occupies exactly the same position as the house mentioned by Sir Richard Cox, Lord Chancellor of Ireland, who in 1687 wrote:

'Donerayle, a sweet seat and a pretty market towne belonging to the heir of Saint Leger, once Lord President of Munster, who kept his Presidency Court here, and had a fine house and a curious park adjoining, but the house was burnt down by the Irish, 1645, and is since rebuilt.'[5]

The basement suggests the present Doneraile Court is an addition to the older house but only the eye of an expert would notice that the upper storey was added in 1725 and the bow windows in the middle of the century. Probably a fire did some damage in 1800 and rebuilding was necessary. In 1830 the porch was added and much later in 1913 an unsightly dining room was built on for a proposed visit of Edward VII. Its beauty and elegance were extolled by one Smith, an 18th-century visitor, who manages to capture the spirit of the great house and the beauty of its gardens as they were then.

'Doneraile is indebted for the greatest part of its beauty to the fine house and extensive improvements of Hayes St. Leger. It is situated on a rising ground to the south-east end of the town, facing the River Awbeg, which is formed into a fine cascade with reservoirs. In the front court, on a pedestal, stands a statue of a gladiator, with other lesser figures. The out-offices are large and regularly built; the gardens well laid out and of a very considerable extent. In them is a wilderness and a labyrinth, and towards the foot of the gardens is a canal of 170 yards long and 140 broad well stocked with fish. The water is constantly supplied by a large wheel that casts up a part of the River Awbeg into a reservoir, which is conveyed underground into the canal, and returns back over a cascade into the road. On the other side of the river are pleasant lawns, and an extensive deer park, well planted and enclosed, and to the east of the house is a fine decoy. Near the bridge to the west end of Doneraile, the river is broad and deep, being retained in a fine basin for supplying the cascades formed by it as it passes the above improvements, and it is adorned with islands, planted with groves of fir, which add an inexpressible beauty to the place.'[6]

By the end of the nineteenth century, set in six hundred acres of fine land and mature woods through which the 'Mulla' flowed, the place was being called Doneraile Park: an army of thirty gardeners tended the gardens. A visitor there in 1853 noted:

> 'Strolled in the gloaming through Lord Doneraile's park. Magnificent old trees, oak especially, noble elms, ash and a Spanish chestnut of fine stems, one of them about sixteen feet in girth. Rabbits in great numbers and comparatively tame. Pretty ponds with swans and a little cygnet.'[7]

But the charm of the place had been recorded long before the nineteenth century by Edmund Spenser who recalls that in Elizabethan times the spot was a favourite venue for Raleigh, Sydney and himself who wandered under the limes or rested in the 'cooly shade of the green alders'. Those born into such fair surroundings were fortunate indeed.

* * * * *

The Honourable Elizabeth St. Leger belonged to the fortunate few. Born to a life of privilege in the elegant milieu of Doneraile, she enjoyed with her sister and three brothers all the blessings and advantages of a favoured eighteenth-century existence. Her education took place in her own home with private tutors; indeed she grew up like any other daughter of wealthy, influential parents whose sole aim was to prepare her for marriage to an acceptable suitor when the time arrived. Her life might have been uneventful and Elizabeth forgotten today had it not been for a curious incident one afternoon in the winter of 1712.

Her father, the first Viscount Doneraile, was an ardent Freemason. Occasionally he opened lodge in a room next to the library at Doneraile Court, assisted by his three sons, Arthur, John, and Hayes. A few close friends would be invited to attend the meeting.

The story goes that one November afternoon, Elizabeth was sitting by the window in the library reading. As dusk gently closed in upon the house, and the words on the page grew dim in the fading light, she fell asleep.

At that time, the alterations and rebuilding of Doneraile Court had not been completed, and part of the wall dividing the library from the adjoining room was being removed to make an archway between the two rooms.[8] Some of the bricks had been only loosely replaced. On this particular afternoon a special Masonic meeting had been arranged in the Lodge Room to confer degrees.

Elizabeth slept soundly until she was awoken suddenly by the murmur of voices. Not wanting to disturb her father's company, she waited quietly for a while, then, succumbing to a natural curiosity, she peered through the cracks in the temporary brickwork through which light from the next room could filter into the library.

The gathering was, she realized in a flash, no ordinary one; mystified by the proceedings she gazed on in fascinated silence. Slowly, the solemnity of the ceremony evoked her fear and apprehension, and a strong sense of being an intruder persuaded her to try slipping away quietly. Her only means of escape was through the Lodge Room itself. Hoping and praying the men would be too engrossed in the ceremony to notice her, she held her breath and glided soundlessly across the darkened far end of the room to the door on the other side. Softly opening it she walked straight into her father's butler, the Tiler of the Lodge, standing on guard at the door with a drawn sword.

Startled out of her wits, Elizabeth gave a piercing scream and fainted, alarming the company inside. She was immediately carried back into the library to explain herself. The Brethren returned to the Lodge Room to discuss what to do next, and after a considerable time had elapsed and agreement reached they summoned Elizabeth to explain the only course left open to them . . . and her. She would have to be initiated as a Freemason if the secrecy surrounding Masonic activities was to be preserved.

She was hardly able to refuse her consent and was instructed there and then about the responsibilities she had unwittingly brought upon herself. She cannot have been more than nineteen at the time. A year later she married Richard Aldworth of Newmarket Court, Cork, a bond which produced two sons and lasted for the best part of sixty years.

Elizabeth remained faithful to her Masonic commitment throughout her long life:

> 'She lived up to the highest principles of the Order to which she belonged. Possessed of considerable wealth, her purse and influence were always at

the command of any Brother in distress and to all appeals, she responded with ready sympathy and large-hearted generosity . . . She was a most exemplary Mason and headed her Lodge frequently in procession . . . No Mason in distress ever turned his back on her magnificent and hospitable dwelling unrelieved.'[9]

Indeed she would allow no-one to poke fun at Masonry and always tried to set an example herself by living up to its high principles, winning for herself the respect and admiration of her contemporaries: 'Thus lived this pattern of female excellence, dispensing like a principle of good, comfort and happiness to all about her.'[10]

She lived to the gracious age of seventy-nine years, well-loved and highly esteemed by her family and friends. When she died, her body was laid in a vault under St. Finbarre's Cathedral in Cork where it rested undisturbed for one hundred years. In 1870, the old cathedral was demolished to make way for a new one, and an eminent antiquarian of his day, Dr. Caulfield, had the opportunity to examine her remains. He describes his discovery with some warmth:

'She was in a leaden shell and in a wonderful state of preservation. She was attired in a dark silk dress, white satin shoes and silk stockings of a similar colour. Her person was comely: her face of a dusky ash colour: her features quite perfect and calm. She had long silk gloves, which extended above the embroidered wrist bands; her bosom was full and large for her age: she wore a white headdress with a full frill round the neck, the plaits of which were not even ruffled.'[11]

Fortune smiled wryly upon her younger son, St. Leger Aldworth, neatly removing three Viscounts Doneraile in his lifetime. The male St. Leger line becoming extinct with the death of the 4th Viscount in 1767, Aldworth was next in line as heir to Doneraile. He promptly assumed his mother's maiden name and the arms of St. Leger, and was then elevated to the peerage, first as Baron and afterwards as Viscount Doneraile of the second creation.

Through her son, St. Leger St. Leger, the Lady Freemason became the ancestress of all the succeeding Viscounts to reside at the Court until 1969. Elizabeth is certainly the only Lady Freemason in Irish history and was possibly the first in the world.

* * * * *

Lord Doneraile may have been a chip off the old Aldworth block; he inherited none of his mother's graces. A despotic landlord and drunkard, heartily despised by his tenants, he was at the centre of an incident which, while having been related in some detail by several writers, lacks any real documentary evidence. Deviating considerably from local oral tradition, the written account relates how Lord Doneraile seduced a village girl and installed her at the Court as his mistress.

In the district lived an old and infirm Catholic priest, Father Neale, who was instructed by his bishop to excommunicate the girl's brother for living openly with another man's wife. His sister complained to her lover, Lord Doneraile, who, blind with fury heightened by drink, mounted his horse and set off with a relative, Captain St. Leger, for the poverty-stricken cabin which the priest called his home.

They arrived to find the priest at prayer. Undeterred, Lord Doneraile, still in the saddle, roared at the old man to come out. Father Neale emerged to face the angry peer who demanded the censure be removed. The priest tried to explain that the matter was beyond his competence and only the bishop himself could lift the ban. Lord Doneraile had heard enough. Shaking with rage he raised his horsewhip and wildly beat the priest and his housekeeper just come out of the hovel to help her master. Extricating themselves from the lashing whip, the old couple crept back into the shelter, shocked and bleeding. For a Catholic to bring an action against a Protestant in those far-off days was unusual enough, but there was no precedent for a Catholic priest bringing one against a powerful Protestant peer of the realm. Where could a Protestant jury be found who would dare to decide in favour of a Papist? Yet, Father Neale, possibly on instructions from his bishop, sought to bring an action against Lord Doneraile for his crime. No barrister could be found who was prepared to accept the brief.

Finally the story reached the ears of the brilliant John Philpot Curran, the young but already renowned star of the Irish bar. Gallantly he offered his services to Father Neale, a courageous gesture which could have meant the end of his career. His powers of persuasive oratory, his wit and eloquence, had already made him a legendary figure in Irish courts of law. This case was to guarantee him a place among the greatest of popular Irish heroes.

Cork was thronged with people who had travelled for miles to be at the court when the case opened. Philpot Curran, faced with an all Protestant jury, appealed to their sense of justice. Describing the incident in great detail he pressed home the bitter comparison between the pious dutiful priest and the tyrannical aristocrat. The jury, he assured them, had the weighty responsibility to see that justice was done to an honest old man, gravely maltreated by a lecherous lord for simply doing his duty.

Cleverly Curran lifted the jury's sights above naked religious prejudice to focus upon the real legal issue. Once he succeeded in doing that, the jury was putty in his hands.

He achieved the impossible; having gained the jury's confidence, he could even refer to Captain St. Leger as a 'drummed out dragoon' and a 'renegade soldier' without losing ground. Deeply moved by such an eloquent presentation of the facts, the jury returned an impartial verdict awarding Father Neale thirty guineas in damages, as much as he earned in a whole year.

The day after the trial, Captain St. Leger, intent on revenge, challenged Curran to a duel with firearms. Standing face-to-face, the Captain invited Curran to fire first but the barrister refused. 'No,' he replied, 'I am here by your invitation, it is for you to open the ball.' The Captain fired . . . and missed. Curran declined to counter-fire, an experience from which the Captain never recovered: shaken to the core he died a few months later.

Curran's last encounter with Father Neale was a happier one. The aged priest died very soon after the trial too, but not before sending for Curran. While the distinguished lawyer stood over him at his bedside, Father Neale explained that since he had neither silver nor gold to reward Curran, he wished to pronounce upon him the formal blessing of the Church as a sign of his everlasting gratitude.

Although the incident was soon swept under the carpet by the St. Legers, the Irish do not forget ...

Local tradition simply holds that the parish priest concerned was not Father Neale but Father John Cotter, parish priest in Doneraile from 1739-1784 whose grave is in the Oldcourt graveyard.

He is said to have preached on the evils of Lord Doneraile's private life as it affected his parishioners. The message of the sermon was repeated to his Lordship by one of his Catholic servants and in his rage he horse-whipped the priest. The burial place of the famous Father Neale in question is unknown, and the Captain cannot be identified in family records, although at the time the family seethed with soldiers. The absence of any documentary evidence of the case in family records may suggest that Lord Doneraile destroyed it himself.

* * * * *

The dazzling opulence of life in the hey-day of great country houses and the stern etiquette observed by their inhabitants has been vividly portrayed by our outstanding novelists.

Life at Doneraile followed the accepted pattern of the age of elegance when the nobility and gentry spent their days in vigorous activity pursued in romantic surroundings. Doneraile Court became the vibrant centre of social life in the area: its foremost attraction was to the sportsman, providing some of the finest hunting, shooting and fishing in the British Isles. The viscounts, all of them enthusiastic horsemen, had at their disposal a large number of splendid mounts stabled at the Court.

Local history records a running match in 1752 between 'Mr. O'Callaghan and Edmund Blake' over St. Leger territory from Butte-vant Church to the spire of St. Leger Church in Doneraile, which had been built by Sir William St. Leger. The run, 'a distance of four miles and half over stiff country,' was the first ever steeplechase. It became a regular event and accounts for the introduction of the word into the English language.

Hunting and racing were favourite pastimes of the viscounts and their families; indeed it is said of the fourth Viscount he only dismounted for a meal and an occasional change of clothing. By all accounts he was a most disagreeable character and became involved in a most extraordinary court case known as the Doneraile Baptismal Suit.

In 1834, the Rev. Somerville was made Rector of Doneraile. He was an idealist and from his induction persisted in preaching sermons which caused the upper stratum of his congregation severe discomfort.

Matters came to a head one day while the Rev. Somerville was taking a walk with the Rector of Ballyclough who was visiting Doneraile. Somerville suddenly caught sight of Lord Doneraile in the distance and exclaimed 'There goes that scoundrel, Doneraile'. Some days later, the Rector of Ballyclough repeated the remark to the Rector of the neighbouring parish of Buttevant (St. Leger territory), a close friend of Lord Doneraile, who lost no time in passing it on.

A few months later, Lady Doneraile gave birth to a child and Lord Doneraile promptly fetched the Rector of Buttevant to baptize the infant. Somerville courageously contended that since the Rector of Buttevant had no facilities for the parish of Doneraile his administering the sacrament had been highly irregular and he put the matter before the Ecclesiastical Court in Cork.

However, the subsequent trial was taken up by a discourse on Somerville's unchristian behaviour in not going to see the Lady Doneraile straight after childbirth. Somerville became the accused not the plaintiff, and the outcome of the case left Somerville without a congregation. The parishioners drifted off to another church about three miles away from Doneraile.

The rift between him and Lord Doneraile widened when one of the Viscount's sons died in infancy and was buried in Buttevant – later to be exhumed and brought back to Doneraile after Somerville had left the parish. The unfortunate man died miles away in 1867, ostracized by his own 'christian' community.[12]

Disagreeable Lord Doneraile may have been, but he hardly deserved his terrifying end. Out hunting with friends one day he was bitten by a fox: the beast had rabies. A coachman too was bitten. It was known to a few that Pasteur was doing research into the disease and its prevention, so the Viscount and his coachman, clutching at the last straw of hope, travelled together to Paris to seek out the great chemist.

Both were treated: only the coachman returned to Doneraile cured, some said because his blood was purer than the stuff than ran in Lord Doneraile's veins. When the madness set in he was locked in an upper room at the Court, but his indescribable suffering drove the family to taking a terrible decision. It was agreed that the gentlemen of the district should administer the coup de grâce; they ascended the two flights of stairs, entered his room and the crazed Hayes St. Leger, 4th

Viscount Doneraile, was smothered by his friends in his own bed.[13]

The family interest in sport was not restricted to hunting. Lord Castletown of Upper Ossory, husband of Lord Doneraile's daughter Ursula, the only child to survive and therefore his heiress, founded the local lawn tennis and croquet clubs in 1910 and the golf club in 1912.

Edward, sixth Viscount Doneraile, devoted much time and energy to organizing the Wimbledon Lawn Tennis Championships over a period of many years. He first served as a member of the Committee of Management in 1905, and was in office from 1911 until the outbreak of the Second World War. Another member of the family, Vere Thomas St. Leger Gould, triumphed in the first ever Irish Lawn Tennis Championships in 1879 and reached the Finals of the All Comers Singles at Wimbledon in the same year. Foolishly, he ruined his reputation by murdering someone in the South of France.

However, sport was not their sole pursuit. As members of the establishment they were obliged to play an active part in the affairs of the town. The church built by Sir William and entirely maintained at the family's expense was the first Protestant church to be erected in Doneraile. The present Catholic church, a large, light and airy building, occupies a site given by Lord Doneraile in 1827 to the Very Reverend John O'Brien, the builder of the Presentation Convent in Doneraile.

The family was unceasingly engaged in the political life of Ireland before and after the Union of Ireland with England in 1800. Until the dissolution of the ancient Irish Parliament at the Union, a member of every generation represented Doneraile in Dublin — hardly surprising considering the franchise was vested only in those freeholders selected by the incumbent viscount. Even after the Act of Union the family continued to influence the way people voted until the introduction of the secret ballot in 1872. .

St. Legers were ever-present in the army, in large numbers. The withdrawal of most of the British army in the 1770s for service in America left the country without a militia and resulted in the formation of the Irish Volunteers. It was a Protestant army commanded by officers drawn from the landowning nobility and gentry who planted themselves firmly behind Gratton's patriotic cause.

It fell to Lord Doneraile to form a company of cavalry which was called the Doneraile Rangers. The elite young gentlemen just couldn't resist the temptation of dressing themselves in a resplendent uniform of scarlet, faced green, edged white, gold epaulettes, yellow buttons and helmets, green jackets, faced red with goatskin! The company's officers in 1782 were Colonel St. Leger (Lord Doneraile) and Major the Hon. Hayes St. Leger, his son and heir.

To their credit they devoted a deal of energy and time to providing adequate educational facilities for the area. In 1817, Lord Doneraile was sponsoring a spinning school; some years later he was lending his support to a Lancastrian Free School for three hundred Protestant and Catholic boys. At the same time a school run by the local Protestant Minister was being entirely maintained by Lord Doneraile. Lady Doneraile financed a small school for girls.

More recently, Lord Castletown, Chancellor of the Royal University of Ireland, figured in 1908 as a prominent negotiator for the establishment of the National University of Ireland. At a local level his genuine interest and help in the work of the Christian Brothers who still run a school in Doneraile, won their appreciation and he is remembered in their *History of the Institute*:

> 'He manifested great friendship and good will towards his Catholic fellow citizens, tenants and particularly towards the Christian Brothers.'

* * * * *

The story of an historic house in Ireland would not be complete without taking heed of its ghosts.

Local tradition once held that when a St. Leger was about to die a red deer would come to the main door of the Court and a coach drawn by headless horses would race through the town. One evening in March 1854, about the time of the 3rd Viscount's death, a local farmer was returning home when quite suddenly he met the coach head on. In front of the headless horses bounded a huge yellow hound.

Yet again, in 1887 another farmer was leaving Doneraile by the Mallow Road, driving his mare and cart when he had an identical experience. His mare, scared out of her wits by the phenomenon, grew so tense and white with foam that he had to return to Doneraile immediately to calm the beast down.

Such tales can always be challenged yet it is hard to dismiss the experience of one of the most reliable witnesses to a supernatural happening in the 19th century, that of one of Lord Doneraile's park-keepers whose story appeared in the *Occult Review* for February. 1906.

> 'One bright night he was coming across Lord Doneraile's park — having been round to see that the gates were shut — when his attention was drawn to the distant baying of hounds, and he stopped to listen, as the sound seemed to proceed from within the park walls, and he knew that there were no hounds kept on the estate. His young son was with him, and also heard the noise, which was getting louder and clearer, and was evidently moving rapidly in their direction. His first idea was that a pack of hounds which were kept in the hunting kennels a few miles away had escaped, and had somehow got into the park, although he had seen that the gates were closed, and there was really no way by which they could have entered. The baying of the hounds, as if in 'full cry' sounded closer and closer, and suddenly out of the shadow of some trees a number of fox hounds, running at full speed, appeared plainly in the clear light of the moon. They raced past the amazed spectators (a whole pack of them), followed closely by an elderly man on a large horse. Although they came very near, no sound could be heard but the baying of one or two of the hounds. The galloping of the horse was not heard at all. They swung across the grass at a tremendous pace, and were lost to view around the end of a plantation. The park-keeper knew that all the gates were shut, and that it would be impossible for a pack of hounds to pass out, and he thought the mystery might be solved the next day. However, it never was explained by any natural cause. No hounds or horsemen had been in the park. The mansion was closed, Lord Doneraile being away, and no one had the right of entering the grounds within the park walls. He heard later that there was a story in the neighbourhood about a "ghost" of a former Lord Doneraile "haunting" the park, and possibly the spectral horseman was he.'

The horseman was thought by the family to be the 3rd Lord Doneraile of the first creation who was killed in a duel.

The 1st Viscount is believed to ride to hounds though the park sometimes, in hot pursuit of a stag: witnesses throughout the years testify to having heard the horn, the barking of dogs and the tramping of hooves as they ride by.

A sadder spirit is of one of Sir William's daughters who fell in love with Roche, a young Irish chieftain. Sir William violently opposed the affair and Roche was killed by Sir William's followers. His heart-broken daughter pined her life away, and one day was found dead on the exact spot where her lover had been so mercilessly slain. Her ghost, 'the white lady' used occasionally to be seen drooping over a wall nearby as evening drew in.

The 2nd Viscount has been seen standing under an ancient oak close by the wall of the demesne, clad in buckskin leggings and hunting costume. At other times he has been seen riding a powerful black horse across country.

A present resident of Doneraile, an expert in local history, recently pointed out that while he had never heard any of the ghost stories confirmed, the red deer did go to the door of the Court at the death of the 7th Viscount in 1956. One thing is certain about Ireland: where there is a ghost, stories abound, and where there is a story-teller, ghosts are in plenty.

* * * * *

Among the most eloquent expressions of civilization are its great houses, yet when an era passes and with it a life style, a house can become more of a problem than a prize. As the movement towards independence gathered momentum in Ireland, Irish-born St. Legers trickled away from the country, some back to England, others to South Africa, New Zealand or the States. An Ireland separated from England spelt the end of a certain kind of existence for the landowning dynasties of the past. With the dawn of the twentieth century their families grew smaller or became extinct, as if the urge to procreate died as the raison d'être was withdrawn.

Following the death of Edward, 6th Viscount Doneraile in 1941, his brother Hugh and his wife Mary had to return from New Zealand, abandoning their successful sheep farm to take up residence at the Court in the absence of a direct male heir. They too had no family, so as early as 1941 some concern arose about Hugh's heir. In a letter dated July 1942, Edward Coulter, a leading Irish Mason, wrote to my grandfather — also a Mason:

'Dear Brother St. Leger,
When Mr. George Hamilton, Agent at Doneraile, Co. Cork, to Viscount Doneraile, was here a few weeks ago he asked me if I could help him to trace Richard St. John St. Leger the next heir . . . He is under twenty . . . Can you help in any way to trace him . . .'

Hugh died in 1956, still ignorant of Richard St. John's whereabouts. Eventually he was found in California working for a trucking company. In 1958 he petitioned the House of Lords claiming the right to vote at any elections of representative Peers for Ireland — the correct procedure for establishing claims to peerages of Ireland. His petition was, in accordance with the usual practice, referred to the Lord Chancellor to consider and report upon to the House of Lords. No such report was made and no details of the case have ever been made public.

Richard's father, Algernon, heir to the title, left Ireland in 1895 for Canada but drifted down to California where Richard was born and brought up. To follow up his claim, Richard brought over his wife and five children to Doneraile, where they stayed in 1969 with the aging Lady Doneraile.

By this time, Doneraile Court, after years of neglect, was in a bad state of repair, and Richard and his family tried to devise ways of raising money for the preservation of the house. In a racily-written article published in the *Washington Post*, January 1969, a vivid description is given of the difficulties encountered by the family in trying to keep the place going. Heating the house was only one of many problems, and Richard junior, a Vietnam War veteran, was having to work on a neighbouring farm.

A serious family dispute arose. The Irish Land Commission had used its statutory powers to institute compulsory proceedings to acquire the property in 1963. As far back as 1943 it had already purchased some 370 acres of the estate, and the Irish government intended to complete the purchase. Objections were raised by the trustees of Edward's will, but were subsequently withdrawn.

Richard St. John St. Leger put his claim for the Viscountcy before the Lords for a decision, but jumped the gun by deciding to open Doneraile Court to the public, advertising the fact in the Irish press. For the opening, arranged for July 1969, the American Ambassador was invited. The surviving trustee of the will of Edward, sixth Viscount Doneraile, acted swiftly by taking the case to the High Court in Dublin. He won. An injunction was granted, restraining Richard and his son from inviting or permitting members of the public to enter the mansion. The decision was based on an expert's examination of the building which was said to be a danger to the public if they were admitted. There was fear of the floors collapsing under the weight of the crowds expected to visit the house.

However, the Land Commission was prepared to do a deal with Richard St. Leger, offering him the mansion and 118 acres of the demesne for £18,000, but Richard failed to agree. The Irish Georgian Society had generously come to his aid by launching a 'Save Doneraile Fund' and their invitation to volunteers to do essential maintenance work on the house had elicited quite a favourable response but in August, 1969, the family decided to return to America and the house was yielded up to the Land Commission.

The dowager Viscountess moved into a cottage nearby only to die a short while later. The contents of Doneraile were sold to dealers, mainly American: many of the portraits of St. Legers and a large collection of objects of real historical value found their way into new homes in the United States. The valuable library went for a paltry sum.

Alongside the usual hunting trophies and arms which decorated the walls of the house were prizes salvaged from long-forgotten battles in Britain's dim yet glorious past: the Tippoo Sultan's silk flag, carried back from Seringapatam; a collection of ornaments from the summer palace in Peking, and numerous other curios from the Far East. Among the reminders of the sixteenth century were two iron treasure chests, painted and ornamented, once cast up upon Tranmore beach and reputed to be part of the wreckage from the Spanish Armada.

Before 1963, Nelson's sword had been kept at the Court and there was a copy of the warrant issued to execute Charles I signed by Cromwell and others. Part of the collection was a box of chessmen carved in bone by French prisoners-of-war and presented by them to Lord Doneraile who was in charge of them during the Napoleonic campaigns. The gift suggests they had been well-treated.

Emptied of its contents the Court stood for several years unused, abandoned it seemed to an inevitable destiny of decay and ultimate collapse. But the Georgian Society of Ireland, ever-watchful of the Irish heritage, stepped in to take over Doneraile Court in an attempt to rescue the building from a sad fate. In May, 1976, the Society was presented with the deeds of the house by Tom Fitzpatrick, Irish Minister of Lands, on condition the house be repaired. The Society pledged to carry out urgent restoration work to save the house from irreparable ruin. An appeal was sent out by the Society for funds and ideas on how to use the house to 'ensure its future'.

Work was started almost immediately. The roof was repaired first at a cost of £10,000 so that the urgent restoration work to the interior could be undertaken in dry conditions. Volunteers offered to mend the windows before the winter of 1977 set in and the Society received encouraging support from residents in the area who arranged several benefits in aid of the house. But more help is still needed if the job is to be finished. Owing to the efforts of a vigilant group dedicated to saving and preserving the Georgian houses of Ireland, a future for Doneraile's historic mansion has been secured.

* * * * *

Doneraile town has kept its character and unspoilt charm: people still have time for one another. A question or two put to Donerailians relaxing in one of the several bars along Main Street elicited elaborate stories about St. Legers of the past.

A picture emerges of a family wielding absolute authority yet who managed to keep themselves remarkably aloof within such a tight-knit community. Some of the men who had worked for the family for over thirty years caught their first glimpse of the Court's inner precincts after the house had been taken over by the Irish Government. Privacy for the viscounts had been a priority. In general they appear to have been just landlords and fair employers — 'all the families for miles around were kept by Lord Doneraile' a Doneraile resident remarked to me; yet was it not Lord Doneraile who was 'kept' by these families?

Their sins were not interred with their bones . . . 'one of their Lordships sired half the town', another man joked. However, the scholarly Callaghan O'Callaghan, a local resident with a phenomenal knowledge of local history (and perhaps the finest private collection of books and documents on the area outside the National Library) remembers their Lordships with a certain amount of affection. Surprisingly free from the resentment one might expect to find in one whose family has had to live for generations as tenants, Callaghan speaks generously of them:

> 'The St. Legers avoided hostilities with the Irish, and I did hear that in the Civil War between the Royalists and Parliamentarians, they wavered for a while before taking sides. They seemed to be good politicians, always able to assess how much they could safely accomplish. Doneraile as I knew it in the early years of this century did accept the St. Legers, at least I was not aware of any hostility towards them.'*

O'Callaghan maintains that today life has become much more complicated. While His Lordship was up at the Court one could approach him with grievances which would be promptly dealt with. Nowadays one fills in a form, sends it off and is lucky if the matter is attended to within six months.

But the Irish always kept their wits about them. O'Callaghan remembers asking an employee of a gentleman who lived in a neighbouring castle why he accepted £1 per week from him when he would want 30/- if he were employed by O'Callaghan. The man explained with faultless Irish logic that he could rob the gentleman while he would never rob O'Callaghan.

The story aptly illustrated the attitude of some people to the gentry, looked upon as 'fair game' by a large section of the community. O'Callaghan believes this will be found in any country where property is so unevenly divided.

Is Doneraile complete now the big house is empty? If stories can keep a family around, the St. Legers will be ever-present in that historic town.

---

*Letter Nov. 1978

SECOND PART

4. The original 'commodious Stand' at Doncaster.

CHAPTER FIVE

THE RACE

ONE day early in 1778, a group of noblemen and gentlemen gathered for a private dinner party in an upper room of the Red Lion Inn which stands in the market square in Doncaster. When they departed, history had been made. A horse race which was to set the pattern for classic racing throughout the world had been christened the St. Leger.

The race, a sweepstake for three-year-olds, had been born two years earlier in 1776, at the suggestion of Lieutenant-Colonel (later Major-General) Anthony St. Leger, and run for the first time over a two-mile course on Cantley Common in Doncaster. At least it has always been assumed that the first run took place on the Common. Not so, say the people of Firbeck, a village near Worksop, and they have a good case. It was run, they claim, on Anthony's private racecourse[1] on the 'oval field' near his home, Park Hill Hall.

A recent Ordnance Survey aerial photograph shows the field quite distinctly and what is more, the distance around the field is approximately two miles. In the centre of it once stood a pump used for watering the horses; later it was surmounted by a plaque commemorating the first event.

However, Cantley Common did provide the main venue for racing in the eighteenth century and the 1776 Doncaster Race Meeting appears in the Racing Calendar for that year. Nevertheless, wherever the original unnamed race was held, the idea of a two-mile test for three-year-olds was in all probability conceived on the oval field: 'once round the field, gentlemen ...'.

Sweepstakes in those days enjoyed widespread popularity. The innovation of the St. Leger had been to run it off in one heat, breaking with English racing tradition of running important races over much longer distances in several heats. At Newmarket for instance, horses contesting the Town Plate would have to cover three heats over the Round Course, a distance of twelve miles with a break of half-an-hour between each heat, hard work for even the hardiest horse. The new St. Leger deviated radically from this tradition. It was agreed that should a dead heat occur a run-off was to be held to decide the winner.

Eighteenth-century racing was patronized chiefly by the nobility and local gentry. One of the greatest sporting peers of the era was undoubtedly Charles Watson-Wentworth, second Marquess of Rockingham who had been twice Whig Prime Minister. While hardly a statesman of great stature his liberal views advocating independence for the American colonies were well-publicized. Had he been a better politician and spent less time on the turf, the American War of Independence might have been averted. But racing claimed most of his attention and as a founder member of the Jockey Club he secured for himself a place in the history of racing while his policies have long been forgotten. Indeed a pun circulating in his own lifetime suggests his contemporaries were not over-impressed by their leader: 'The Ministry sleeps and the Minister's Rocking'em'.

The Marquess entered two horses for the new race planned for Tuesday 24th September, 1776. Three other owners including Anthony St. Leger also subscribed to the sweepstake of twenty-five guineas for each horse entered. Rockingham's filly ridden by John Singleton junior won. At that time it was customary for racehorses to be identified only by colour, sex and pedigree since the names of their noble owners were considered of prime importance. Consequently, Rockingham's winning filly received her name, Allabaculia, much later when it had become common practice to give horses names of their own.

Allabaculia seems a curious choice of name for a filly since the real Allabaculia was a swashbuckling oriental adventurer, Ali Bey Kuli, who had led a revolt in Egypt aimed at forming a new Egyptian ruling dynasty. The failure of his venture led to his death but his story fired the imagination of English high society for whom he became a hero for a brief period; he would certainly have been forgotten long ago had his namesake not headed the result list of the first St. Leger:

>   Lord Rockingham's br. f. by Sampson — 1
>   Mr. A. St. Leger's br. f. by Trusty — 2
>   Mr. Wentworth's b. c. Orestes by Doge — 3
>   Lord Rockingham's ch. c. by Remus — 0
>   Mr. Foljambe's b. f. by a son of Blank — 0

Two days after the initial event, a meeting at the Mansion House — the Mayor of Doncaster's official residence — approved the proposal that the racecourse should be moved from Cantley Common where it was agreed the gentry could not be accommodated comfortably enough. It was resolved to establish a new racecourse on Town Moor and to erect a new 'commodious stand' for onlookers. The minute from the meeting on September 26th, 1776, states:

> 'Ordered, that the setting out and direction of making a New Course for the races on Doncaster Common, and a Commodious Stand, shall be referred to the Marquis of Rockingham, Peregrine Wentworth, esq., James Farrer Esquire, Anthony St. Leger Esquire and Childers Walbanke Childers Esquire.'[2]

The moving of the course from Cantley Common which extended southwards from the southern boundary of Doncaster Common was unavoidable. The decision to shift its location narrowly preceded the enclosure of Cantley Common for which an Act of Parliament was passed in 1777.

Carr, a reputable architect, was commissioned to build the new stand plus additional stabling. He did the job for a mere £2,637, earning for himself one hundred guineas. The present racecourse lies more or less in the same position as the one of two centuries ago.

The race evoked so much interest and excitement that it was run again the following year. Before the September 1778 meeting, the story goes that the stewards of the Race Club, together with the Mayor of Doncaster, Alderman Rickard, and some distinguished owners and supporters, met at the Red Lion to discuss the stakes for the meeting.

The subject of a name for the new race was raised and someone suggested it should bear the name of the most prominent person present – Lord Rockingham. But his lordship demurred, remarking, 'it is my friend St. Leger who suggested the thing to me: call it after him'. While no concept of a classic yet existed, the Marquess had unknowingly named the first of its kind.

From its inception the St. Leger has always been run in the September Race Week, fixed in the eighteenth century as the principal meeting held at Doncaster. The race was not a particularly notable event in its early years but by the beginning of the nineteenth century it had become one of the major attractions for sportsmen throughout the land.

Very gradually the racing world recognized the truth of the old Yorkshire saying, 'the fittest horse wins the Two Thousand Guineas, the luckiest horse wins the Derby, but the best horse wins the St. Leger'. Indeed it is the supreme test of stamina, late enough in the season for three-year-olds to have attained maturity, and certainly a more telling contest than the French Grand Prix de Paris run over one mile, seven furlongs, earlier in the racing year.

Initially the events of the race week at Doncaster were patronized predominantly by people and horses from Yorkshire and the northern counties. As rumours of the success and popularity of the St. Leger Stakes filtered slowly through the land, racegoers from all social classes and every region in Britain made their way to Doncaster. They came on foot, in humble carts, on horseback or in ornate carriages. The gentry flocked into the town, renting the fine houses for the September Race Week and the Town Council made every conceivable effort to entertain the visiting nobility and gentry in style. There would be hunting in the morning, racing in the afternoon and a lavish choice between glittering balls, entertaining supper parties or the theatre for the evening's amusement. The New Betting Rooms near the Mansion House catered for the gambler; cock fights and prize fights drew large crowds hungry for the excitement of contests in the ring.

Thousands of pounds were laid in bets on horses running in the St. Leger. The scale of betting which started months before the race produced enormous problems. By July 1806, over a million guineas had been laid in bets for the St. Leger that year; the question remained, how many betting losses were paid. After the races of these early years the sight of levanters clambering on to any train, whatever its destination, was a familiar one.

The Race

Doncaster has a history of infamy. Villains, rogues, tricksters and cheats arrived each September in hoards intent on interfering with horses or bribing the jockeys. False starts were engineered to irritate highly-strung thoroughbreds: in 1813 no fewer than ten false starts frustrated the St. Leger's runners. Swindlers swarmed into the town, bent on cheating the merry crowds where they could.

The Doncaster Corporation grew increasingly concerned about the racecourse getting a bad name and consistently tried to maintain some semblance of order during the St. Leger Race Week. But the problem stumped them in 1829 when the military had to be summoned to disperse a band of hooligans armed with rough clubs and threatening to march on the town. Eventually order was restored.

In later years the Doncaster police force, assisted by units of the West Riding Constabulary, kept order, whilst detectives from London and elsewhere were drafted to Doncaster for St. Leger week to keep track of travelling pickpockets and card sharpers, in town to make a dishonest fortune from unsuspecting racegoers.

The rail link to Doncaster completed in 1849 brought huge crowds to the St. Leger meeting. The privilege of seeing the now famous St. Leger which had until then belonged exclusively to the wealthy and to local Yorkshiremen was now extended to all interested in the sport. Thousands more could now witness for themselves the race of which was written in 1831:

> 'The great St. Leger crowns the racing year — to it all minor ones succumb. It resembles the premiership or the wranglership in academic honours. We may safely say that no event throughout the year causes such intense speculation, or creates more interest among all classes.'

For thousands of Yorkshire miners and their families in the late nineteenth century, St. Leger Day was celebrated as an annual holiday. The pits closed down and the race would be attended by a sea of spectators in cloth caps. York racecourse attracted the fashionable and would be decorated with masses of flowers: the Doncaster course had much larger crowds and heavier betting.

'The Doncaster St. Leger', remarked one nineteenth-century observer, 'is run in the presence of a crowd of critical experts, amongst whom the racehorse is the object of as much serious worship as the cat, the ox, or the crocodile was to the ancient Egyptian'.

As the popularity of the race grew Doncaster shopkeepers and market traders did a booming business, and pubs overflowed with racegoers drowning their sorrows or celebrating their victories on the turf. Owners of large houses let them at exorbitant rents to house parties, bookmakers and jockeys: St. Leger week kept the rouble rolling fast, an aspect of the meeting hardly changed today.

Notable changes took place in other quarters. Doncaster betting odds and racing results, nowadays transmitted within a fraction of a second by radio and television, travelled slowly in the early years. That in 1836 the result of the race travelled the fifty-eight miles from Doncaster to Manchester in two hours, twenty minutes, was considered then to be speedy. Later, pigeons were used to spread the news of racing results; the first time a result was flown all the way to London by pigeon post was in 1825 when Memnon won the race. By 1843 the practice had caught on, and the biggest flock of pigeons ever released from Doncaster spread the news of Nutwith's victory all over Lancashire and Yorkshire.

Probably the greatest change to have taken place since the founding of the St. Leger has been in horse transport. Racehorses of those early years would be expected to walk from one course to another; a journey from Newmarket to Doncaster could take up to six weeks, exposing the horse to all manner of discomfort and even infection on the way.

Then the winner of the 1836 St. Leger made turf history. Elis, a useful colt belonging to Lord George Bentinck, had been entered for the St. Leger but was still being worked at Goodwood shortly before the September Meeting. With the St. Leger approaching and Elis still at Goodwood, the punters assumed the horse would not reach Doncaster in time. Bentinck, whose tactics had in the meantime lengthened the odds, commissioned Herring the London coach builder to build an enormous wagon roomy enough to transport two horses in relative comfort. In this very first horse-box, drawn by six hefty horses, Elis and another horse, The Drummer, were taken up to Doncaster travelling at the astonishing speed of eighty miles a day. Elis arrived in fine fettle, proving by his win the success of a venture which marked the beginning of a new era in racing.

The idea soon caught on everywhere. Elis's journey was nevertheless a far rougher one than a present day thoroughbred experiences. It travels in a luxuriously equipped box (often more comfortable than the car towing it) along smooth, fast roads to ensure it arrives at Town Moor in a fit and rested condition before competing in the event.

Over that stretch of Yorkshire turf have ridden the noblest horses and the greatest jockeys of all time, competing year after year in the toughest test for three-year-olds.

William Scott, Frank Buckle, Fred Archer, Nat Flatman, Tommy Weston, Charlie Smirke, Gordon Richards and Lester Piggott have all taken winners past the post. The list of horses includes the finest the world has ever seen: Orville, The Flying Dutchman, West Australian, Gladiateur, Ormonde, Isinglass, Flying Fox, Diamond Jubilee, Gainsborough, Bahram and Nijinsky, evocative names in the story of English turf.

Owners have ranged from noblemen to scoundrels, all English until 1865, when for the very first time the race went to a foreign horse and owner. The French Gladiateur was owned by the most notable and respected personality of the nineteenth-century French racing scene Comte Frédéric de Lagrange. With so many horses entered by foreign owners in today's big races it is hard to conceive the degree of humiliation suffered by English racing enthusiasts at the foreign St. Leger win of 1865.

English confidence had been severely undermined by the brilliant colt's successes in the 2000 Guineas and the Derby; that he should add the St. Leger alarmed the English considerably. The French gleefully celebrated their Triple Crown victory over their old rival. The event opened up a new age for the St. Leger. Baron de Rothschild was the next foreign owner to take the prize with his filly Hannah in 1871. What is more the Baron walked away with four of the five classics that season.

The first member of the Royal Family to win took the race with Persimmon in 1896. H.R.H. the Prince of Wales had already won the Derby that year and incredible scenes of wild jubilation greeted his victory. Another of his horses won again in 1900, completing a Triple Crown victory. It is fitting that the first-ever photograph of a St. Leger winner is that of Persimmon standing with his bowler-hatted royal owner.

The British prefer their great races to go to royalty: King George VI added a further St. Leger win for the family in 1942 and the Queen delighted the Doncaster crowds gathered to see the race in Silver Jubilee year by winning with Dunfermline, a splendid start to the third century of St. Leger.

Royalty have been visitors to the St. Leger since 1806 when the race was attended by the Prince Regent and his pleasure-loving brother who later ascended the throne as William IV. Princess Victoria attended in 1835 as a guest of Lord Fitzwilliam but it was Edward Prince of Wales who brought royal romance to the race by starting the tradition of entering royal horses. His were hardly surprise wins, his horses were first-class.

Yet there have been some startling victories, none more so than the one of 1822. Jackson, who with his eight St. Leger wins must rank among the greatest jockeys of two centuries, experienced a moment of utter despair before the start of the race that year. He was to ride Theodore who was lame. It certainly was not the first time a jockey had mounted a horse without a chance; the crunch came when he was instructed to ride to win. Jackson burst into tears.

Thoroughly frustrated, Theodore's owner, the Hon. E. Petre, sold all his bets to a Mr. Mills for £200. The odds against Theodore winning lay at 1000 to 5 yet the sturdy steed was in front from start to finish and won by a magnificent four lengths. Mr. Mills went home that night a rich man.

In 1803 a lame jockey won. Benjamin Smith, winning jockey in six St. Legers of the nineteenth century, started his career on the wrong foot — or rather, with a broken leg. It happened at the start of the race when a horse kicked him, making his win on Lord Strathmore's Remembrancer well worth remembering.

* * * * *

Two centuries after its modest beginnings, the race is still drawing vast crowds to Town Moor. The 200th running of the St. Leger was celebrated on September 11th, 1976, with that inimitable English flair for combining dignity with fun and, for the first time in almost two hundred years, St. Legers were involved. Julian St. Leger, whose ancestors had lived at Park Hill, presented the trophy. Reports about the Race's long and vivid history, on television, radio and in the press, reminded the public of the event's importance as the significant turning point in racing history. The story of its beginnings was related in lectures, and for museum-goers in Doncaster, a carefully-compiled exhibition encapsulated the town's racing connections.

Firbeck too celebrated. Members of the local History Group mounted an exhibition in the parish church and villagers revelled a week long on the old stamping grounds of squire St. Leger. The merry-making began with a Country Fayre on St. Leger Day; on the Sunday the Bishop of Sheffield preached at a special service in the church and at the end of the week the festivities culminated in a St. Leger supper for all comers.

Embroiderers too were busy. As of old when historic events were recorded with needle and thread, a Bicentenary Tapestry, designed by Joan Cooke and Edith John, slowly took shape under their needles and those of their helpers, Olga Catterson and Margaret Stephens. The work, now displayed at each St. Leger Festival, depicts all the outstanding St. Leger winners of the last two centuries.

Beautiful commemorative objects were produced too. Bell Brothers, an old-established Doncaster firm of gold and silver-smiths, chose to remember the occasion with two superb silver goblets. Her Majesty the Queen was presented with a pair of them on St. Leger Day. Royal Crown Derby produced a classic bone china vase for Francis Sinclair of Doncaster, decorated with a hand-painted illustration of the first St. Leger.

The official trophies commissioned by the Doncaster Corporation were a fine Wedgwood plate showing Tattersall's painting of the 1846 St. Leger and a Coalport Eagle Vase with a hand-painted reproduction of J.F. Herring's painting of the 1825 winner, Memnon.

The morning of St. Leger Day saw the same upper room of the Red Lion, venue of the 1776 dinner party, crowded with guests come to join the Mayor of Doncaster, Councillor Gallimore, at breakfast. As did his eighteenth-century predecessor, he too sits on the Racecourse Committee and that morning he moved among famous owners, trainers and jockeys exchanging racing talk over a specially concocted 'St. Leger Coffee'. At noon the Queen arrived, after a long absence from

Doncaster, to see Mr. Wildenstein's Crow ridden to victory by Yves Saint-Martin. Her presence eloquently completed the historic scene.

Anthony too hit the headlines. Unaccountably the Red Lion had never had an inn sign hanging outside the house. The occasion of the Bicentenary provided the ideal opportunity to rectify the matter. A reward of one hundred guineas was offered by Berni Inns, the proprietors of the Inn, to any person who could produce an authentic picture of Anthony St. Leger which could eventually be incorporated into a new inn sign to swing above the entrance. To bridge the gap, a temporary sign was presented at the party by Mr. Jim Pearce, Managing Director of the chain in which the Red Lion is now a link. It promised:

REWARD
100 Guineas
FIND
Anthony St. Leger

The search was on. The offer, given wide coverage in the British and Irish press, elicited a number of responses from people living at home and abroad, each of them drawing attention to the portraits by Reynolds and Gainsborough of Anthony's nephew, John Hayes St. Leger. No picture of Anthony has yet come to light.

The Bicentenary spirit sent the Doncaster Racecourse Manager, Don Cox, and his wife Audrey, to France and Germany. They visited the racecourse in Dortmund to see the 92nd running of the Deutsches St. Leger. For the first time in Germany a member of the St. Leger family presented the trophy to the winning jockey, J. Pall, who had ridden Stuyvesant — from the Schlenderhan stables — in a hard race against the British jockey Eric Eldin, riding Countess Oettingen-Wallerstein's horse Tuttlinger.

Anthony surely would have smiled with approval had he known that one day English and German turf lovers would raise their glasses together in a toast to him, as they did after the race that day in September 1976.

The bicentenary of the naming of the race in 1978 was not overlooked. A plaque outside the Red Lion was unveiled by the author in the September of that year. Directly afterwards Mayor Winifred

Liversidge J.P. presided over a small group of guests gathered once more in the upper room for a commemoration dinner. The Bicentenary was complete.

Every country in the world with a tradition of racing eventually adopted Anthony's idea: Hungary, Ireland, Italy, France, America, Japan, Australia, New Zealand and Chile. Yet the indefinable ambience of a particular afternoon in September each year on Town Moor is unique to the English St. Leger. If the never-ending saga of the Doncaster classic comprises all the elements of a great epic, it is because from the very beginning of man's relationship with the horse there has been memorable achievement, romance, excitement, scandal and sometimes tragedy. A race simply concentrates all these elements into a few breathtaking moments.

Yet the St. Leger is not just another race: its sheer antiquity gives it the edge on all races in the world. The Derby, its most illustrious offspring, may claim more attention nowadays, nevertheless anyone fascinated by classic racing is aware that, like Adam, the St. Leger is the father of them all.

Presumably Anthony and his fellow members of the 1776 Race Committee never imagined how the event would develop. By 1824 the crowds had outgrown the 'commodious stand' which had to be extended by a further storey to provide accommodation for a thousand more spectators.

Today's crowds on Town Moor for St. Leger Day are no smaller. They still prefer to mingle in the colourful scene with its atmosphere of speculation and excitement rather than lounge lazily before a television screen. But there, Doncaster spoils its racegoers: the racecourse, one of the finest in Europe, lays on every modern facility both for racing and the comfort of its spectators. A new grandstand with roomy restaurants replaced the old stand in 1969, once the finest of its time.

A whole racing circus is required to stage the St. Leger and its back-up programme. The framing of the race involves entries being gathered in, the forfeit stage and finally the declaration to run. Technical services play a vital role nowadays, the photo-finish camera, the camera patrolling equipment; as do the race officials, including the man in charge of the Weighing Room and the stipendiary stewards. Hiring of casual labour takes the regular staff of twenty-five well beyond two hundred at the time of the St. Leger Festival. The catering complex alone has a turnover of more than a quarter of a million pounds.

No pains are spared to achieve perfection for the St. Leger: on the morning of the Bicentenary run, Don Cox was testing the turf at four o'clock in the morning. By the time the eager crowds stream down Leger Way to the Grandstand hundreds of man hours will have been spent in preparation.

And so it goes on year after year, each St. Leger adding yet another page to racing history and a new legend to be unfolded over a pint at the ancient Red Lion Inn.

Doncaster Racecourse Committee 1776

His Worship The Mayor — Alderman Rickard
Alderman Halifax
Alderman Holmes
Alderman Whitaker
Mr. James Jackson
Mr. Woodcock
Mr. Dunhill

Doncaster Racecourse Committee 1976

His Worship The Mayor Councillor G. Gallimore, J.P.
Chairman — Councillor A.E. Cammidge, J.P.
Vice Chairman — Councillor R.W. Gillies, J.P.
Councillor E.L. Adams, B.A.
Councillor E.H. Bailey
Councillor P. Carmody
Councillor A. Haywood
Councillor J.E. Oliver
Councillor I.W. Prior
Councillor H. Schofield
Councillor Mrs. O. Sunderland
Councillor M.C. Welsh

Doncaster Race Club Committee 1776

Lord Rockingham
Peregrine Wentworth, Esq.
Childers Walbrooke Childers, Esq.
Lt. Col. Anthony St. Leger

Doncaster Race Club Committee 1976

Earl of Scarbrough
C.D. Naish, Esq.
H.B. Marshall, Esq.
S. Bowman, Esq.

5. Park Hill, the seat of Major General Anthony St. Leger, from a mid-19th century lithograph.

CHAPTER SIX
THE PEOPLE OF PARK HILL

THE only facts to be gleaned about Anthony from reputable works of reference are his military rank and the name of his home. Indeed the wealth of recorded historical detail and modern reportage available on the race, contrasted with the dearth of information about its founder, appears to provide sufficient evidence to support the old notion that the British think more of their animals than their fellow men. Wholly justifiable, some will argue, in the case of the noble horse. But who was the horse-loving soldier of Doncaster?

Anthony, nephew of the 1st Lord Doneraile, baptised in 1731 in County Kildare, was the fourth of five sons born to Sir John St. Leger of Grangemellan, Baron of the Irish Exchequer. After his education at Eton and Peterhouse, Cambridge, faithful to the accepted pattern of the day, Anthony followed his brothers into the army. At twenty-two he held the rank of a sub-lieutenant in the 2nd Troop of Horse Grenadiers, the start of a long and successful army career to which he devoted thirty-two years of his life.

He was a dedicated soldier but nevertheless vivid memories of his rural childhood kept alive his love of country life and he took a growing interest in farming as time went on. In 1761 he married a Yorkshire girl, Margaret Wombwell, co-heiress to the large Wombwell estate. By 1762, he had risen to the rank of Lieutenant Colonel in the 124th Foot.

The following year brought an act of Providence. The regiment was disbanded and with no further regimental appointment forthcoming, Anthony was suddenly free to devote all the time he wanted to his second love — farming.

He took his wife to live at Firbeck, a small village between Worksop and Doncaster, where he purchased the Park Hill Estate, a fine sporting property on which stood an elegant Georgian mansion, Park Hill Hall. Anthony increased the estate to five hundred acres by purchasing adjoining land, the estate and the Manor of Laughton. The Hall included extensive servants' quarters, a brewery, a butcher's shop and stabling. The St. Legers became quite self-sufficient in their village home. Settled in the depths of the rolling Yorkshire countryside Anthony undertook serious agricultural research with the aim of improving farming methods in the district.

For most of the country gentlemen of the period, horse-racing provided a perpetual source of exciting entertainment. Throughout the land races were held regularly at a local level. Doncaster had a long history of the sport in which Anthony, a keen horseman, showed an avid interest, so keen in fact that he had a private racecourse laid out in a field adjoining the estate.

His association with racing at Doncaster is first recorded in 1763 — the same year as his regiment disbanded — when he was successful in the £50 plate at the September race meeting. The race which was to bear his name was born at a time when Anthony was taking an active interest in the newly-formed Jockey Club, to which he was a subscriber, although the St. Leger racing colours were never registered.

Not only did Anthony lend his name to the 1776 event, the name of his estate has also been perpetuated by the Park Hill Stakes, founded in 1837, and also run at Doncaster.

Anthony's interest was not confined to outdoor pursuits. The local theatre attracted him and he made friends with Tate Wilkinson, a popular 18th-century actor. Through Anthony's influence Wilkinson was granted the lease of the New Theatre in the market place, built by the Doncaster Corporation and opened for the first time the day before the first, then as yet unnamed, St. Leger of 1776.

Politics too claimed his time and energy between 1768 and 1774 when he sat as M.P. for Grimsby.

The halcyon days of life as a country gentleman could not last for ever; he was first and foremost a soldier. In September 1779 Anthony was given another regimental appointment as Colonel of the 86th

Foot. As Brigadier-General he saw active service in St. Lucia, commanding troops defending the tiny but strategically important island during the Caribbean struggle of 1781. His promotion to Major General and a post of Staff Officer in Ireland marked the end of his discreetly distinguished career. On 19th April, 1786 he died in Dublin and perhaps the short inscription on his tomb in St. Anne's best sums up the man:

> In every station in life
> He merited the highest approbation.

On Anthony's death Park Hill Estate passed to his nephew, John Hayes St. Leger, whose name is also associated with the race. John enjoys the dubious honour of being the family rake. While the exploits of a rake usually scandalize his own generation, stories of his debauchery, embellished by the imaginative details added by the storytellers, provide an everlasting source of delight and amusement to future generations.

John, born in 1756 in Grangemellan and educated in England and France, spent some time at the Court of the ill-fated Louis XVI acquiring a taste for decadent amusements and consorting with the most enchanting courtesans of the age. On his return to England he joined the army and by 1778 was Captain in the 55th Foot in whose uniform he was painted by Sir Joshua Reynolds the same year.

While still a young man he struck up a close friendship with the Prince of Wales who chose him to be Groom of the Royal Chamber. To mark the occasion, the Prince commissioned Gainsborough to paint two portraits, one of himself and the other of John.

The paintings are so similar in composition and style that they suggest Gainsborough was carrying out a specific request of the Prince to emphasize their shared features. When the portraits were completed, the Prince presented John with the one of himself while retaining that of his friend: it still hangs in Buckingham Palace. The portrait of the Prince was transported up to Park Hill and hung alongside Reynolds's portrait of John until the middle of the nineteenth century. Both paintings now hang at Waddesdon Manor in Buckinghamshire.

Of John's Irish friends, Whaley, a famous eighteenth-century libertine, must have been the most eccentric. Together they revived the

Hell Fire Club in Dublin, on one occasion setting fire to the apartment where they had been drinking just to see how long they could endure on earth the flames they expected to engulf them throughout all eternity. On other occasions it is said they celebrated the black mass.

John possessed a roving eye and did not hesitate to exploit his good looks when in pursuit of game. The Duchess of Rutland, wife of the Viceroy in Ireland, readily surrendered to the charms of 'handsome Jack' and became his mistress. His affair with her was common knowledge.

Once after a dinner given in the Dublin home of the Duke and Duchess, John noticed his beloved washing her hands and cleaning her teeth. He called for a glass, filled it with the water the Duchess had just used and flamboyantly drank it down to the amusement of the assembled guests.

The Duke, eying his rival with disdain, remarked wearily: 'St. Leger, you are in luck Sir; her Grace washes her feet tonight. You shall have another goblet after supper.'[1]

Either John grew tired of debauchery or he grew up. By all accounts he later became a more likeable and responsible member of the Prince's set. Possibly increased responsibility in the army and political duties bred a late maturity in him. In 1795 he sat as M.P. for Okehampton, Devon. An army posting took him out to Trincomalee in Ceylon as Commander-in-Chief but he disappears from Army Lists in 1801.

Since John had remained a bachelor, Park Hill was inherited by his brother, Anthony Butler St. Leger, married to Harriet Chester who had come from another renowned Yorkshire family. Their only son, Anthony Francis, inherited the property at his father's death, but died unmarried.

The problem posed by the absence of a direct heir was solved by passing Park Hill to Harriet's nephew, John Chester, who assumed the surname and arms of St. Leger in lieu of his own by Royal Licence in April, 1863.

He served his country well. Following a distinguished army career in the Shropshire Light Infantry he returned to take up residence at Park Hill and his duties as a J.P. and Deputy Lieutenant of Yorkshire. Like so many old soldiers injured during service – he had sustained severe wounds in the Battle of Sobraun for which he received the Medal and

1. Ulcombe Church.

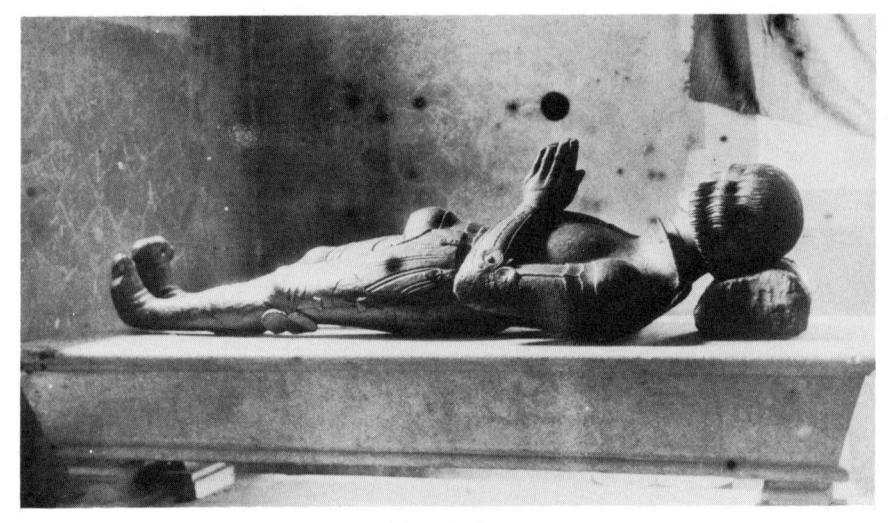

2. Sir Anthony St. Leger, Slindon Church, Sussex.

3. The Ros tomb, St. George's Chapel, Windsor.

4. Sir Richard Grenville (unknown artist after a portrait of 1571).

5. William Warham, Archbishop of Canterbury (1503-32), after Holbein, 1527.

6. *(left)* The arms of Henry VIII and Queen Catherine Parr; *(right)* the arms of Sir Anthony St. Leger at Leeds Castle.

7. Leeds Castle.

8. (*above*) John Philpot Curren by Sir Thomas Lawrence.
9. (*below*) Doneraile Court in the snow.

10. The Lady Castletown of Upper Ossory. Painting by Frank Brook, *c.* 1906.

11. Hayes St. Leger, 4th Viscount Doneraile (1818-87). From an oil painting at Doneraile Court by Weigall, R.A., 1861.

12. The 'oval field' north of centre.

13. (*above*) Doncaster Races, 1830. An oil painting by James Pollard, showing the improved stand of 1824

14. (*below*) The Marquess of Rockingham (by a student of Reynolds).

15. John Hayes St. Leger by Sir Joshua Reynolds.

16. John Hayes St. Leger by Thomas Gainsborough.

17. The Hon. Elizabeth St. Leger as a girl.

18. The Hon. Mrs. Elizabeth Aldworth: The Lady Freemason (wearing the Freemason's Apron).

19. Early *Cape Times* premises.

20. *Cape Times* premises in 1978.

21. Frederick York St. Leger, the 'Old Saint'.

22. Grandfather Frederick York.

23. Don Cox and Herr Miebach at the German St. Leger in Dortmund, 1976.

24. The author presenting prizes at the German St. Leger, 1976.

25. (*left*) Royal Derby Commemorative Bicentenary Vase.

26. (*below*) St. Leger Stakes Bicentenary Commemorative Plate by Wedgwood.

27. (*above*) Presentation of Bicentenary Wedgwood Vase, showing Julian St. Leger (*left*) and Mr. D. Wildenstein (*right*), owner of Crow.

28. (*below*) Unveiling of plaque at *Red Lion*, September 1978. From left to right: Brian Marshall (Doncaster Race Club Committee), two representatives of Berni Inns, Moya Frenz St. Leger, Mayor Winifred Liversidge, Donald Cox (Racecourse General Manager) and Mayoress Mavis Smith.

29. (*above*) Today's Grandstand at Doncaster.
30. (*below*) Find Anthony: new inn sign for *Red Lion*.

Clasp — he kept silent about his handicap.

The house and estate remained in the family until Major Bonfoy St. Leger sold up in 1909.

It was never easy to find new owners after that. The whole character of the district had been changed by the building of a colliery and the old rural way of life was disappearing. However, a new use for the house was found. In 1913 the buildings were being used as a girls' school, but later on, ownerless once more, the house became the meeting place for the villagers of Firbeck who played whist in the dining room and held regular dances in the drawing room. The floors were kept highly polished by a local resident who recalls that she used 'grated candle-grease and large quantities of elbow grease to do it'.[2]

In 1930, the house and estate were up for sale again, advertised quaintly as 'originally the home of the St. Legers, one of whom, Colonel St. Leger, was the founder of the famous race which bears his name'. The advertisement continues confidently:

'The estate comprises a sporting property of 500 acres situate for the most part in the pleasant neighbourhood of Firbeck . . . Firbeck and the adjoining township of Letwell are practically unchanged and unspoilt, and form a most pleasing contrast to neighbouring villages which have become industrial centres. The locality has many associations with the old families of Gally Knight, the Jebbs and the Whites of Wallingwells, and is an ideal neighbourhood in which to spend a country life. It is a typical sporting district, and no doubt, in days gone by, many a sturdy disturber of game has been laid by the heels and put in the stocks still preserved in Firbeck churchyard.'

A buyer was found; in 1935 he pulled the house down. Had it survived another decade or two, into the era of the conservation-conscious, it seems certain that the house would still be standing today. However, part of the kitchens and the servants' quarters were converted into a house: the brewery, the butcher's shop, the original stables and a portion of the walled garden can still be seen.

The land is now owned and farmed by a prominent member of the local community, J. Batty, Esq., J.P., who remembers the Hall as it was. Not all trace of some racing beginnings in Firbeck has vanished: close by the St. Leger memorials and stained-glass window in Firbeck Church hangs an apt reminder of the man whose name makes the sporting headlines each year . . . a racing bridle.

6. Major Barry St. Leger and Chief Thayendanega

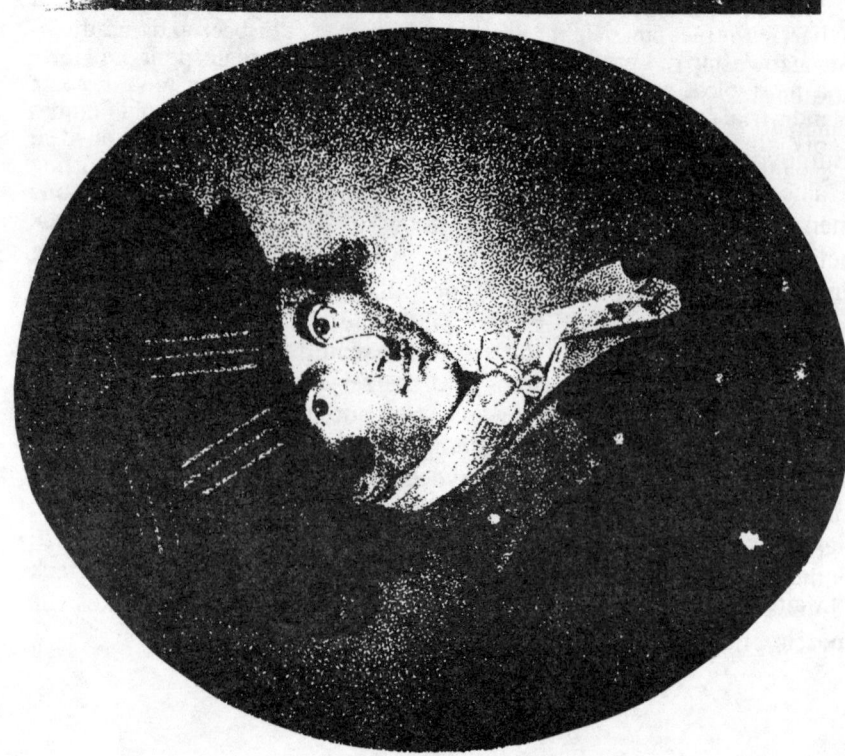

CHAPTER SEVEN

THE AMERICAN WAR

MAJOR Barry St. Leger, one of Anthony's four brothers was, at the time the race was taking shape, attending to another British priority — battling in Canada against the American rebels in their War of Independence.

Barry had been despatched by his Commanding Officer, General Burgoyne, to lead an expedition of loyalists and Indians by way of the St. Lawrence River to Lake Ontario, to win back for the British a strategically vital stronghold, the formidable Fort Schuyler, which had fallen to the rebels. It was planned that he should eventually rejoin Burgoyne further south in Albany, and continue the campaign together.

The army under Barry's command consisted of seventeen hundred men including Indians led by Chief Thayendanegea: all sincerely believed Fort Schuyler would surrender without resistance, frightened by the widespread rumours of Burgoyne's military strength.

The Indians, co-opted for an alien cause in somebody else's war, were of doubtful loyalty. They could only be relied on to obey orders if they saw some advantage for themselves in so doing, and thus presented Barry with something of a problem. Whereas the British troops could be relied on to obey marching orders, not so the Indians. One of Barry's officers records a typical incident during the long march:

> 'The seventy or eighty Messesauges had stolen two oxen from the drove of the army, and would not advance but stayed to feast. I advanced without the Indians seven miles further . . . Set off next morning at six, having waited for the savages till that time, though none arrived.'[1]

Pressing on with his depleted forces, Barry arrived at the Fort and laid siege, assuring his officers that he wished 'to prevent the barbarity and carnage which will ever obtain where Indians make a superior part of a detachment'. The result of the siege proved that Barry had seriously underestimated the spirit of the garrison. Fortunately for them, reinforcements and provisions had arrived a few hours before Barry's army surrounded the Fort, strengthening the garrison's determination to hold out, whatever lay in store.

Barry's initial tactics were to send in a flag together with a pompous proclamation full of threats and lavish promises designed to make a strong impression on the garrison:

> 'The forces intrusted to my command are designed to act in concert, and upon a common principle, with the numerous armies and fleets which already display, in every quarter of America, the power, the justice, and, when properly sought, the mercy of the King.'

The statement continues in a moralizing tone denouncing,

> 'the unnatural rebellion which has already been made the foundation for the completest system of tyranny that ever God in his displeasure suffered for a time to be exercised over a froward and stubborn generation. The arbitary imprisonment, confiscation of property, persecution and torture, unprecedented in the inquisitions of the Roman Church, are among the palpable enormities that verified the affirmation.'

After accusing the rebels of the 'profanation of religion' and the civil authorities in rebellion of many 'shocking proceedings' he then strikes a magnanimous note.

> 'Animated by these considerations, at the head of troops in the full powers of health, discipline and valour, determined to strike where necessary, and anxious to spare when possible, I, by these presents, invite and exhort all persons in all places where the progress of this army may point, and by the blessing of God I will extend it far, to maintain such conduct as may justify me in protecting their lands, habitations and families.'

To those who would join his standard he offered employment, to the infirm and industrious, security, and for all supplies anyone could bring to his camp, he promised payment in coin. But in concluding he warned;

> 'If, notwithstanding these endeavours and sincere inclinations to effect them, the frenzy of hostility should remain, I trust I shall stand acquitted

in the eyes of God and men, in denouncing and executing the vengeance of the state against the wilful outcasts. The messengers of justice and of wrath await them in the field; and devastation, famine, and every concomitant horror that a reluctant, but indispensable prosecution of military duty must occasion, will bar the way to their return.'[2]

Barry's splendid threats were made in vain. The garrison commanders were unimpressed, and every officer and man was determined to defend the fortress to the bitter end.

Hostilities began almost immediately and Barry notified General Burgoyne of his action, unaware of the distressing circumstances in which his Commanding Officer found himself at the same time. Indeed, the news of Barry's advance encouraged him to change his tactics at a critical moment in the campaign. The Americans, on hearing of Barry's position, were quick to react. A relief party made up of militia and gentlemen volunteers sped across country towards Fort Schuyler. Their advance was impetuous and disorderly. No precautions were taken, no flanking parties formed and no scouts were sent forward to reconnoitre the ground ahead of them. They rushed along, an undisciplined mob; an ugly fate awaited them.

When he learnt of the relief party's approach, Barry laid an ambush: a body of soldiers with a strong force of Indians lay in wait at a spot cunningly selected by Chief Thayendanegea. The trap was a path crossing a deep ravine, marshy at the bottom. The road was completely commanded by the hills on either side covered by dense woods, and the unsuspecting Americans walked into the snare.

All the feelings of hate, revenge and resentment stored in the breasts of men engaged in that most passionate of the wars — civil war — were released upon one another on that fateful day. The English fired as the Americans advanced, then jumped out on them from the woods, attacking with their bayonets. Others died from the blows dealt by the butts of muskets and from knife wounds inflicted in savage fury. Severed heads rolled and blood flowed as the Indians massacred indiscriminately. In hand-to-hand fighting, one man throttled another, driving in a dagger at the last moment to finish off his gasping victim. This barbarian bloodbath was considered at the time to be one of the severest and most bestial battles in the whole of the Revolutionary War. British records state that four hundred Americans were slaughtered and two hundred taken prisoner. An eye witness described the battlefield in the wood as he saw it some days later with horror.

> 'I beheld the most shocking sight I had ever witnessed. The Indians and the white men were mingled with one another just as they been left when death had first completed his work. Many bodies had also been torn to pieces by wild beasts.'

The siege continued and Barry sent a further message into the Fort demanding surrender, but the garrison stood its ground. Barry moved his ordnance nearer, firing all the time.

Then an extraordinary thing happened. A brilliant American *ruse de guerre* brought about the complete and utter failure of Barry's expedition.

The trick had been the idea of the American General Arnold. Waiting with his forces at a neighbouring fort for his battle to begin, he sent an Indian emissary into Barry's camp wearing a garment riddled with bullet holes. First he went among the Indians pointing to his clothes to demonstrate how narrowly he had escaped from the approaching rebel army. When asked about the number of troops involved he simply pointed upwards to the leaves on the trees. The report spread like wildfire through the camp sparking off a mass exodus of Indians.

Barry sent for the intruder to his tent and interrogated the man, whose story failed to convince him. The Indians, making their precipitate flight did not tarry to listen to Barry's repeated attempts to reassure them, but in the tangle of the hasty retreat captured and murdered soldiers of their own army, stripping them of guns and ammunition. By plundering several of the army's boats, they were able to escape down the river.

Barry's threats of savage vengeance sent only a few days earlier into the American garrison cannoned back on his own forces — such as were left. So ended the siege of Fort Schuyler, an event heralding General Burgoyne's own ignominious defeat at Saratoga exactly two months later. Barry joined Burgoyne for the final battle on October 7th, 1777 when the British army was forced to surrender to the new Americans.

A fortuitous connection exists between the loss of America and the birth of classic racing. Burgoyne returned to England a broken and dispirited man. Soon after his arrival in London he had to face a motion against him in the House of Commons. Immediately, he requested a court martial believing this to be the honourable thing to do in the circumstances; it was however refused him.

His misfortunes had begun in 1776 when his wife, Lady Charlotte, daughter of the 11th Earl of Derby, had died. Utterly dejected after that calamitous year, Burgoyne moved back to his old home. The Oaks, originally an ale-house he had bought and fitted out as a hunting lodge and later sold to his wife's nephew, the 12th Earl of Derby.

How does a depressed yet otherwise eminently practical man cope with a critical period in his life? Generally he makes an effort to turn his mind away from grief to activities which appear to hold out some promise of relief. And so it was with Burgoyne. He was a known racing enthusiast and a long-standing friend of Major General Anthony St. Leger.* Both knew Sir Charles Bunbury who had owned race horses for years and held office as a steward of the Jockey Club to which Anthony subscribed. It is not inconceivable that Burgoyne or Bunbury, or indeed both men, were up at Doncaster to see the experiment with three-year-olds run on Town Moor in 1778; certainly rumours of the competition had by then filtered south, and the event would have been discussed at the Jockey Club.

In 1778 there was an experiment in evening racing at Epsom, breaking with the long tradition of morning and afternoon heats, an incredible strain on the horses. This meeting may have sired the Oaks and the Derby, but it is far more likely that the St. Leger's success exerted a more direct influence on the founders of the Epsom classic.

The race at Doncaster had interested Bunbury and undoubtedly Burgoyne too, having been founded by his old army friend. Burgoyne is believed to have persuaded his wealthy and influential young nephew to try out the Doncaster idea over Epsom turf, and at a party at The Oaks in 1779, Lord Derby, Bunbury and others agreed 'over Lord Derby's curious port' to run a race similar to the St. Leger at Epsom. This one was to be for three-year-old fillies, racing over a one-and-a-half

---

*Burgoyne was also a personal friend of Lord Rockingham who appointed him C. in C. in Ireland when the Whigs returned to power in 1782. Major General Anthony St. Leger was already there as Staff Officer.

mile course, to be decided in one running only. It was appropriately named after its birthplace, The Oaks; its success as a brief, brilliant event packed with all the excitement and tension evoked by fast racing and heavy betting echoed that of the St. Leger.

The following year yet another race, this time for three-year-old colts over one mile, was staged at Epsom and called the Derby, an event to become the gem of the racing year. There can be little doubt that the idea for these two world-famous classics and the pattern of classic racing throughout the world took shape from the example set by the soldier of Doncaster.

* * * * *

Barry returned to England with General Burgoyne, lucky to have escaped with his life. His cousin, Hayes, a Captain in the 63rd Foot, was less fortunate in that futile struggle for King and country. A couple of years later he sustained fatal injuries when in September 1781 a force under Lt. Col. Stuart saw action against General Greene's men in Eutaw. Hayes died of his wounds in Carolina, four weeks later.

Yet another cousin served as a Cornet, carrying the colours for the Dragoons in America; he too was injured. Only Brigadier-General Anthony St. Leger, founder of the Stakes, saw a short-lived victory much further south on the Caribbean island of St. Lucia, where he was Military Governor. The tiny island, so unimportant a spot in peacetime, became vital for military operations and naval manoeuvres in time of war, when the British West Indies were forced to enter the war.

War against the American colonies spelt disaster for the islands of the Caribbean, and up to the last moment everything was done in London by those with West Indian interests to avert the catastrophe, to no avail. When it came, the British West Indians had to decide where their loyalties lay — a sticky choice since, as in North America, opinions and loyalties were divided.

The British West Indians shared many of the same grievances nursed for so long by the American; they too had protested violently against the Stamp Act, borne the heavy burden of taxation and fermented with the injustice of having no real legislative freedom. Yet, there was one essential difference between the situation of the North American colonies and the rich, vulnerable Indies: defence. Whereas the rebels rejected the notion that they needed British protection for which they had to pay so dearly, the British West Indies knew they would be lost without the aegis of the Royal Navy. Therefore, despite the persistent attempts of the revolutionaries in the north to win over the Indies for their cause, the southern island colonies refused to join in the war. But it was impossible for them to be bystanders for long.

France's recognition of the New American Republic in 1778 was smartly followed by a declaration of war against Britain. Spain followed suit in 1779. While both nations entered the war chiefly to fight side-by-side with the rebels, this was by no means their sole purpose. The revolution provided an ideal pretext for pillaging British possessions in the Caribbean. The islanders suffered from a multiplicity of hardships during the period and fighting brought trade to a virtual standstill. Worse still, they were cut off from supplies of basic commodities, bringing the people to the brink of starvation.

Circumstances deteriorated even further when two severe hurricanes and a massive tidal wave wreaked havoc over the islands. Planters, short-handed on the plantations owing to the abnormally high death rate amongst the slave population, could not get their sugar away. Chaos reigned. The highly desirable islands enclosing the Carribean sea became the scene of repeated naval and military skirmishes between the three powers and it was not long before Barbados and Jamaica were struggling in the grip of commercial strangulation.

The Royal Navy, already stretched to its limits to provide support for the British armies fighting in North America, was hardly in a position to blockade the French ports in the Caribbean. The French and Spanish fleets could attack either in North America or in the West Indies whenever they wished to; their superiority at sea was unchallenged for long periods. The situation looked irreversible.

A turn in events came in September 1778. When the French after repeated onslaughts took Dominica, the British retaliated three months later by capturing St. Lucia, strategically perhaps the most important island in the Antilles. For the French the loss was a serious one and the British were determined to retain the island at all costs. It possessed four of the largest and safest bays in the West Indies:

Cul-de-Sac, Castries, Choc and Gros-îlet, all ideally situated within view of Fort Royal in Martinique, the main naval base of the French. The power in possession of St. Lucia could command the whole of the archipelago. The military forces on the island in 1781 served under the command of Brigadier-General Anthony St. Leger. By this time, the seas all around were dominated by the Royal Navy, under Admirals Rodney and Hood.

From the invincible fortress of St. Lucia the British were able to reverse their position, and attacked the enemy in every part of the Antilles, harassing their fleets, seizing their convoys, attacking their fortresses and besieging their ports. Baffled and exasperated, the French commanders sent to Europe for naval reinforcements, and resolved to strike a decisive blow against St. Lucia.

Taking advantage of Admiral Rodney's temporary absence from the island in May 1781, the whole French fleet of 25 vessels set out from Fort Royal Bay under the command of the Comte de Grasse and surrounded St. Lucia. A large body of troops landed and took possession of Gros-îlet. The French military commander, the Marquis de Bouillé, demanded immediate surrender threatening 'every severity of war' should the islanders refuse.

'But his threats were received with the contempt they deserved and he was soon convinced that his vanity was not likely to be gratified by the capture of that island, by the British opening from the batteries a heavy fire upon the enemy's fleet, which continued until seven of them were compelled to cut their cables and retreat leeward.'[3] Admiral Rodney was swiftly informed of what had happened and a detachment of several fast sailing ships was sent to inform the Royal Navy's commander on the island, Lieutenant Millar, that Admiral Rodney was speeding to his aid. Fortunately His Majesty's ships, the Thetis, the Sancta Monica, the Sybil and the Scourge arrived quickly and 'their presence greatly contributed to the preservation of the island'.

St. Leger was asked in what way the Navy could best help him on this occasion and he suggested the ships should come immediately into Carénage Bay. During this operation, the Thetis struck a rock and sank, a grave setback but even so, not all was yet lost.

It was decided that detachments of the seamen and marines should be landed from the ships without delay. This accomplished, the action could begin. 'The cheerfulness and alacrity with which these troops marched on this service raised the spirits of all around them, and animated them to exert themselves in making an obstinate resistance. The vigilance of General St. Leger at this moment of difficulty and danger was extremely conspicuous and proved that he was well qualified to discharge the important duties he had to execute; and the ardour of the troops could be equalled only by the same disposition which displayed itself in the officers and seamen of His Majesty's ships.'[4]

The professionals were not battling alone. Planters, merchants, masters of trading vessels and their crews, all of them climbed the hills to take up the posts assigned to them. Ironically, many were French inhabitants of the island standing alongside the British against their own countrymen. 'The whole force seemed animated with one spirit, and the effects of this spirit the enemy would have experienced, if they had dared to put their threatened attack into execution.'[5] But they retreated, to the astonishment of the garrison. Moving silently back to the beach, they re-embarked in the night, returning to Fort Royal in such a hurry that they were forced to leave behind on the island much of their baggage which included a large quantity of ammunition.

This unequivocal victory for the British heralded a complete reversal of the misfortunes sustained in the Caribbean struggle. The final triumph of the Royal Navy came in April 1782 at a spot between Guadeloupe and Dominica, when Rodney and Hood attacked the fleet of de Grasse and forced him to surrender. Impoverished and exhausted, the French gave up the fight for the Caribbean, and agreed under the terms of the Treaty of Versailles, to return all the British territories taken during the war.

But, contrasted with the loss of the American colonies, the Caribbean victory brought small consolation to the British, who were left no alternative but to be satisfied with the only good to come out of the war: the return of the men to their families. Anthony St. Leger went home with the rest to a quieter life in Ireland.

TALES OF PASSION:

LORD LOVEL'S DAUGHTER.

THE BOHEMIAN.——SECOND LOVE.

BY THE AUTHOR OF "GILBERT EARLE."

IN THREE VOLUMES.

VOL. II.

LONDON:
HENRY COLBURN, NEW BURLINGTON-STREET.

MDCCCXXIX.

7. The title page of Francis Barry St. Leger's book *Tales of Passion*.

CHAPTER EIGHT

POETRY AND PASSION

AS traditional social structures gradually disintegrated in the wake of nineteenth-century industrialization and the growth of towns, an ever-diminishing number of St. Legers opted for traditional careers as landowners, soldiers or ministers of the Anglican Church. Their inherited responsibilities melted away with social change and, in common with others of their class,* they found themselves on the threshold of an existence where new opportunities and a wider range of choices were presented.

The English gentry had the great advantage over their continental equals in having been prepared for change. It was an exclusive class yet hardly an exclusive life: it had always cultivated universal interests which had kept it in touch with the community as a whole and preserved it from freezing into a separate entity. The nineteenth century offered St. Legers and their kind a liberation from the thousand years of duty-bound rural life. They emerged from their country houses brushing the stable straw from their boots and turned towards the City or left for the colonies, to face new challenges and take up new duties.

One of the first to flee the predictable life of the manor house and the character it stamps was Francis Barry Boyle St. Leger, nephew to Hayes, 2nd Viscount Doneraile. He was born in September 1799, and at an early age showed all the signs of possessing a lively imagination and a quick intelligence. A precocious child, he soon became the

---

*the formal sense of landed gentry.

favourite of his father's circle of friends, a galaxy of talents whose political sympathies lay unequivocally with the Whig Party, Lord Guilford, Sheridan, John Kemble, the famous tragedian who for many years managed Drury Lane Theatre, and many others known for their wit and genius. Francis absorbed from this sophisticated company their liberal ideas and developed an independence in thought and action which stood him in good stead for the future. Sheridan and Kemble dazzled the boy with words and wit, laying within him the foundation for his own chosen career.

His schooldays spent at Rugby could not pass quickly enough for him. Indeed his time there did little more than leave behind a distinct impression that public school education was not the only means of obtaining knowledge, an opinion he consistently argued. The world, he maintained, is the school where education is completed, a conviction which persuaded him to pack his bags and leave for a 'high situation' in the civil service in India.

He did not stay long. The life was repugnant to him, offending his principles and his sensitivities: the habits of the service, the methods of trading and system of government ran counter to his strict sense of justice and his belief in basic human rights. Unable and unwilling to be party to what he felt to be the ugly exploitation of a people, Francis returned to London and to raised family eyebrows. The wisdom of sacrificing a highly lucrative post, a certain fortune and a life of ease for a few thorny principles confused St. Legers of a more practical vein.

Francis wanted an honourable career, so began studying for the Bar to which he was called as a member of the Inner Temple in 1827. Yet his mind, hyperactive from childhood, demanded more stimulation than law studies could provide. Francis turned to writing, adopting his second name, Barry. In 1821 a book of his poems was published. *Remorse and Other Poems* express a deep-rooted melancholy and a longing for past innocence. The poems, aimed at the heartstrings, undoubtedly drew tears from the eyes of his own generation, with their blatantly sentimental nature dealing with such topics as death, guilt, mourning, unhappy love and remorse for acts committed in careless moments. Some of the poems strike a moral note. In the first verse of his long poem *Remorse* he lifts a warning finger:

Yes! I have well deserved the fate,
The woe which you compassionate;
Guilt and remorse have wrought the pain
Which rends my heart and sears my brain.
Oh! if our sufferings here may prove
Atonement for our sins, above —
If these avail, then even I
May dare to look with hope on high. —
If thou should'st ever feel the power
Of Passion's wild and fearful hour, —
If it should tempt thy steps to stray
Beyond the straight and even way,
And break through Virtue's sacred laws —
Think on my story then, — and pause.[1]

The impressions of a writer seeking to release pent up emotions permeates this first attempt at poetry. He appears through the medium of his early poems to be labouring under the colossal weight of a death wish, the only desirable exit from 'sin, sorrow, guilt and remorse' and 'the misery of a lot like ours'.

STANZAS

Oh! that this life of woe were past,
And I were in my grave at last!
That this seared heart, and throbbing head,
Reposed in their sepulchral bed!
There would my sins and sorrows cease,
I there should be, at last, in peace.

There I no more should feel the force
Of love - sin - sorrow - guilt - remorse.
My wearied spirit there would rest,
For there the thought would leave my breast,
Of all the passions wild which moved me,
Of her I loved - of her who loved me.

Yes! were I dead, it would not be
A sin for her to think on me —

> She then might shed a guiltless tear
> For him who living, held her dear,
> And pray the guilt might be forgiven,
> Of all his wrongs towards her, and Heaven![2]

For a young man of twenty-two, such melancholy augured ill for the future.

By 1822, Francis was editing the fashionable annual, *The Album* and contributing wittily-written articles to the principle periodicals of his day. *Gilbert Earle*, his best-known work, was a great success, earning him the praise of the public and the critics. Another novel followed swiftly, *The Blount Manuscripts*, and in 1829, *Tales of Passion*. Reviewing these books the *New Monthly Magazine* commented:

> 'the works are characterized by intense feeling, a thorough insight into human nature, the development of the passions of the mind and a complete knowledge of the world. Such are the works as could be produced only by a man of genius.'

One of the *Tales of Passion, The Bohemian*, tells the tragic story of an idle, French-bred German Count who spots a beautiful and talented Bohemian gypsy dancer at the Leipzig Fair, and takes her under his roof to cultivate her talents and school her in the arts. A precursor of Pygmalion? Hardly. She is abandoned by the Count after a long love affair, and most of the story is devoted to how she seeks her revenge.

As with all his stories, the plot is designed to create a framework for a most detailed study of human emotions, and, as was usual among writers of his day, he quotes widely from the classics as well as French and English literature to illustrate his points.

While the scene of the tale is set in Germany, Poland, Italy and France, the descriptions of these places are scant. The weight of the writer's concentration rests upon his characters and their inner conflicts. Had Francis lived in the twentieth century he would probably have been a student of psychology rather than law. The Bohemian is interspersed with Francis's observations about the human state and man's feelings, but he also has a few remarks to make on education.

> 'In most persons, who are educated at all, the progress of education and

the formation of the character go hand in hand. The mind and the heart advance toward maturity together, and are both acted upon by the food which they consume — which like that of the body, is continually, though unconsciously, becoming part of the system.'[3]

However, understandably for a young man, most of Francis's effort is put into describing and analysing love and passions since, as he observes,

'The craving of the soul to love is one of the strongest and most firmly planted needs of humanity: its endeavours to be satisfied will be violent and frequent, and if it is not satisfied the 'void in the breast' will ache indeed; *naturam expellas furca, tamen noque recurret.*'[4]

Yet clearly Francis is suspicious of love and is ever at pains to draw attention to all the fallibility and weakness which are its pitfalls.

'It is seldom that when the heart is warmed and touched, the reason can remain firm and cool.'[5]

And of love turned to passion he admits,

'In the throes of tumultuous passion, the agitation of the soul is too vehement to admit that softness, that yearning of the spirit, that sweet abandonment of self in which true tenderness consists.'[6]

Passion, he suggests, closes the mind to beauty.

'But upon a heart which the sterner passions fill, the glories of art and of nature — the pomp of historic recollections, and the visible presence of the legacies of genius — will fall alike unheeded. When the mind is occupied by any of the stronger sensations to which it is subject, truly it forms to itself its own world. We look upon external objects, even when they are such as these, with a cold and indifferent eye — our sight is cast always inward.'[7]

Acutely conscious of the conflicts and pain caused by love, Francis asks why it is that love, which should be 'the instrument of joy and happiness' is so often 'the minister of agony and death. Why is it that love which should breathe nothing but blessings, becomes the parent of curses? Why are our best feelings the generators of our deepest crimes?' Small wonder then that Francis can speak so convincingly of despair, 'the most dreadful of all the suffering sensations of the human soul. It is when sorrow assumes the character of despair that it dries up the current of our blood, and makes us old before our time. When hope is absent — when there is nothing left for us to expect or desire, then it is that the frame partakes of the decrepitude of the heart'. Sober words for a man in his twenties.

Yet his attitude towards love was not all wariness. He could write sensitively of the tender moments too.

'Of the power, the magnificent power of the voice of one we have loved, I need not speak. It lives in the heart although unheard for years, and if, after their lapse, it suddenly speaks again, it thrills through us with a shock which checks our blood and respiration, and renders the whole frame trembling, unnerved and powerless.'[8]

Whether in his wittier writings, castigating an impertinence or satirizing a folly, or in his serious articles denouncing a vice or protesting against injustice, Francis seems to have written always with the good of his fellows in view.

In addition to writing and his arduous law studies he somehow found time to undertake research into the history of the Moors in Spain. But his overactive mind was sapping his physical and emotional stamina, and in June 1829 he suffered a seizure. Doctors diagnosed epilepsy. Stubbornly Francis continued his work on the Moors, reading and writing into the early hours nights on end. His friends tried to prevent him overstraining himself — to no avail. Even his doctors were baffled by the problem of how to restrain him from over-taxing his mind. Relapse followed relapse and the inevitable happened on November 20th, 1829, when, in the home of close friends Francis collapsed and died. He was thirty years old. His untimely death put an abrupt end to the flowering of his literary talent, just beginning to take shape by the time his last work, *Tales of Passion*, was published: the writing is altogether simpler and less florid than in his previous works. 'In literature', states his obituary, 'his works place Mr. St. Leger in no mean rank among his contemporaries . . .' An overstatement perhaps considering his contemporaries were Sheridan, Shelley, Keats, Byron, Coleridge and Sir Walter Scott. Yet his life lasted for too short a time to judge whether he might have joined their ranks one day. In the legal profession, his source of income, he was certainly doing well and 'giving evidence of such success in his circuit, as in time would have most probably led to eminence . . .'[9] Albeit, it is doubtful whether Francis would have stuck to law had he lived long enough to emerge as a writer of consequence in his generation. The generous closing words of the obituary summon up the image of an intense, imaginative young man, vibrant with energy.

> 'Barry St. Leger had a powerful mind, strong original conceptions, and a habit of thinking for himself that gave great originality and force to everything which emanated from him, either in writing or in conversation. He was a man of warm but few attachments, and was himself greatly beloved in the circle in which he moved. As a social and intellectual companion in the common intercourse of society, or more particularly in that of his intimates, his qualifications were of the higher order. His powers of conversation were exceedingly great; and a remarkably retentive, as well as discriminating memory, enabled him to illustrate his remarks in a manner that rendered his colloquial intercourse eminently pleasing to those who enjoyed it.'[10]

Broad hints of the brooding melancholy afflicting his spirit and casting its shadow across so much of his writing, suggest his short life was suffered in a state of chronic depression relieved only by occasional moments of animation. Why Francis should have had to bear such a heavy sense of sinfulness is a mystery.

> My heart hath known the fiery force
> Of Passion's wild and fearful hour ——
> In turn, sin, sorrow, guilt, remorse,
> Have cursed it with their withering power.[11]

The transience of passion and the inexorable ensuing torment cracked his fragile frame and will to live. Francis's tragedy was irreversible.

> Oh! it is not in passion's power
> To give one truly happy hour;
> A while, a little while, we seem
> To taste of Rapture's short, short dream;
> But scarce sufficient does it last,
> To shew 'tis real, ere 'tis past;
> And then, alas, we wake again
> To certain grief, to lasting pain,
> Twas thus with me — the joy I knew
> Was desperate — but transient too:
> My grief, my pain are with me still;
> They pass not, and they never will.[12]

THE CAPE TIMES
AND DAILY ADVERTISER.

Vol. I. No. 1.   Cape Town, Monday, 27th March, 1876.   One Penny.

Messrs. H. Jones & Co.'s Auction Sales.

IMPORTANT SALE
OF THE ESTATE
KLEIN WESTERFORD.
This Day (Monday), 27th March.

THE Magnificent Estate of "KLEIN WESTERFORD," situate at Rondebosch, facing the Main Road, and extending to the Newlands Oak Avenue, comprising an all Pid-es Acres of Land, will, in consequence of the Owner's increased official duties rendering him unable to give proper attention to the Property, be put to Auction as above. The whole of the Land is under cultivation; the Vineyard, which consists of about 25,000 choice Vines, gave the season a handsome return, and an inspection will prove them to be equal to it one of Mr. ALEXANDER LORD'S or TORR'S Model Vineyard which Vineyard adjoins this Estate. The soil is known for its richness, and the vegetation of this neighbourhood surpasses in luxuriance any part of this southern extremity of South Africa. In addition to the Vineyard, "KLEIN WESTERFORD" has all the makings which make it a most desirable Gentleman's Estate as well as a profitable Agricultural Investment. There is a fine Orchard, with almost every variety of Fruit Trees of the choicest kind; an extensive Kitchen and Vegetable Garden; a plot of Lucerne, which, like everything else here, thrives wonderfully well; a handsome Paddock with a rich carpet of grass all the year round; and the whole of this Property is fenced on the Wire, and has for hedge rows of the Oaks. Rondebosch and its neighbourhood is of world wide renown for the beauty of its sylvan scenery, and "KLEIN WESTERFORD" is situate in the very centre and in the most beautiful part of it. To describe the scenery properly would fill a volume; to see is better than to read, therefore come to the Sale.

THE BUILDINGS are in perfect order. The House has been newly papered and painted, and contains a spacious Hall and Eight Large Rooms, Drawing, Dining, Break-ast, Bed, and Bath-rooms, Closet, Two Servants' or Out-rooms, Kitchen, Pantry, and Dairy.

IN FRONT OF HOUSE a well laid-out Flower Garden, stocked with a variety of valuable and Choicest Plants and Shrubs, including Camelia Japanica Trees.

OUT-BUILDINGS: Coach-house, Servants' and Harness Rooms, Stabling for Six Horses, and also for Six Cows, Forage Loft, Fowl-house, Pig-stye, &c., &c.

FURNITURE: consisting of the usual HOUSEHOLD FURNITURE, such as Drawing-room Suite, Horsehair Couches, Chairs, Fine-toned Harmonium, Square Piano, Drawing and Dining-room Tables, Pictures, Glass and Earthenware, Kitchen Utensils, &c.

OTHER MOVABLES: Dairy Dishes, &c., Farming and Garden Implements, Alum and English Leather Harness, Saddlery, Chaff-cutter, about 3,000 lb. Keerbery Oathay, Thoroughbred Kerry Bull, 6 Pigs, &c.

STOCK: Three Superior Cows, two in Milk and one about to Calve, 2 Heifers, 1

The Land has been Sub-divided into Building Lots, and plan will be exhibited on Day of Sale.

BONUS AND REFRESHMENTS.
SALE OF MOVABLES WILL COMMENCE AT 10.

J. J. DE VILLIERS, D. A. Son, Agent for the Sale.
H. JONES & Co., AUCTIONEERS.

NOTICE.
To Connoisseurs, Hotel-Keepers, &c.

SOLOMON BROS & CO.,

Who are retiring from the Wine and Spirit Business, have instructed Messrs. H. Jones & Co. to sell by Auction, without Reserve, the whole of their Superior Stock of WINES, SPIRITS, LIQUEURS, FIXTURES, &c.,

To-Morrow, Tuesday, 28th instant,
AT HALF-PAST 2 O'CLOCK,
AT No. 26, STRAND-STREET.

N.B.—S. B. & Co. have some of the best Stukvats in South Africa for Private Sale, at less than Cost Price.

TO HOTEL-KEEPERS.

THE Undersigned, duly authorised thereto by Mr. Hawegner, who is about giving up Hotel-keeping, will cause to be sold at "the THATCHED TAVERN," Green-

TO-MORROW, TUESDAY,

Sundry HOUSEHOLD FURNITURE, of the usual description, Clock, Pictures, Stoves, &c., &c.

A Magnificent BILLIARD TABLE, with Ivory Cues, Rests, Marking Board, &c.

Also, BEER ENGINE and sundry other Articles, too numerous to particularise.

Sale to commence at 10 o'clock.

H. JONES & Co., Auctioneers.
Cape Town, 27th March, 1876.

In the Estate of the Rev. QUINN, Military Chaplain, deceased.

MESSRS. H. JONES & CO.
WILL SELL AT THE CASTLE,
ON WEDNESDAY, MARCH 29,
THE WHOLE ASSORTMENT OF
Dining, Drawing, and Bed-room Requisites,
INCLUDING A COTTAGE PIANO, &c.

SALE AT 10 O'CLOCK.

C. VAN BLOMMESTEIN,
Attorney-at-Law & Notary Public,
WORCESTER.

C. G. AKERBERG
IS NOW LANDING
EX BARK "SAGA,"
DIRECT FROM SWEDEN:

SWEDISH COOKING STOVES, improved Patent, of all sizes
   "   IRONING STOVES, do., do.
   "   PARAFIN STOVES, do., do.
   "   PLOUGHS, Single and Double Furrow, Nos. 4 and 5
   "   MATCHES, "Tandstickors," and "Safety," in 50 and 25 Gr Cases.

ALSO ON HAND,

AMERICAN PLOUGHS, Nos. 19, 21, 25, 26, 75, and Hillside
LUMBER AND SWEDISH FLOORING BOARDS
STINKWOOD AND WAGONWOOD, of all descriptions.

FOR SALE AT LOWEST MARKET PRICES.
No. 3. Strand-street.

A. L. SNELL'S
WINTER STOCK
WILL ARRIVE
ON OR ABOUT THE 10TH APRIL
Grave-street, 1876.

WINTER GOODS

THE UNDERSIGNED ARE NOW LANDING
THEIR
FIRST SHIPMENTS OF THE ABOVE
ALSO,

Bar, Hoop, & Galvanized Iron, all sizes

AND A GENERAL ASSORTMENT OF
IRONMONGERY.
L. H. TWENTYMAN & Co.

WILSON & GLYNN
HAVE RECEIVED,
EX 'GOLDEN FLEECE,' 'RAPIDO,' 'CAPE CITY,' AND 'IRAZ'
LARGE ADDITIONS TO THEIR STOCK OF

OILMAN'S STORES, &c.,
CONSISTING OF—

Gorgona Anchovies		Stearine Candles	
Pickled Salmon		Sperm do.	
Red Herrings, in tins		Paraffine do.	
Do. do. in kegs		Fine and Coarse Oatmeal	
Dutch Pickled Herrings		Pearl Barley	
Lock Fyne Pickled Herrings		Chicory, "Taylor's"	
Herrings a la Sardine		Split Peas	
Salmon, in tins		Sardines	
Bottled Fruits		Swiss Milk	
Jams, 'Morton's'		Sago Seed	
Fancy Confectionery		Biscuits, in bulk, cases	
Keiller's do.		Do. in 22-lb. tins	
Jujubes and Pastilles		Do. in 3-lb. tins	
Packing and Tea Papers		Ground Cocoa	
Blanched Ginger		Salad Oil, in half-pints.	

Glassware and Crockeryware, &c.

EX 'WALMER CASTLE':
Currants—Sweet Milk Cheese—Lard—Compton's Hams and Bacon.

EX 'LILLA' AND 'ZULU':
700 Pockets and Bags Natal Sugars, various shades and qualities.

FOR SALE—LOWEST RATES.
CORNER OF STRAND AND LONG-STREET

ROYAL MAIL SERVICE.
ATLANTIC LINE.

THE following Ships are appointed to leave Her Bay on a Monday in England during the month of March, 1876:

KIMBERLEY, Capt. JOYNER, 8th, calling at St Helena, Ascension, and Madeira.

ROMAN, Capt. SMITH, 15th, calling at St Helena and Madeira.

TEUTON, Capt. BAINES, 22nd, calling at St Helena and Madeira.

One of the Cabins can be seen, and all information as to Freight or Passage obtained, on application to the Company's Agents,
         WM. ANDERSON & Co.

DONALD CURRIE & CO'S
COLONIAL MAIL PACKETS.

For England, calling at Madeira.

DONALD CURRIE & CO'S splendid Line of Clipper Steamers will leave Table Bay at 4 p.m. on the 14th of every month, from the 7th of March, and Dartmouth on the 23rd of each month.

Carry a Purser and Stewardess.

The Cabins are large and well ventilated, and fitted with every convenience.

For further particulars, apply to
     ANDERSON & MURISON.

WANTED

A BEDROOM, Furnished or Unfurnished. Price no object if in a respectable neighbourhood.—Apply, by letter, to 78, Long-market-street.

WANTED

A FRONT ROOM for an Office. Price no object if in a good part of the Town.—Apply, by letter, to 78, Long-market-street.

WANTED a few GOOD and RELIABLE COMPOSITORS, who will be liberally dealt with.—Apply at the Colonial Printing Office, Castle-street.

THANKS

TO the Gentleman who so kindly assisted me in saving my Property on the night of the Fire at St. George's-street.
       T. BRENNEN,
Osborne Hotel, Market-street.

WHITFORD'S
Berlin Wool and General Fancy Shop

IS REMOVED to 21, BURG-STREET, nearly opposite Messrs. Hunter, Arnold, & Co., where a Splendid Stock of NEW GOODS, in Wools, Beads, Canvas, Slippers, Scarves, and numerous other Articles connected with the Fancy Trade, are for Sale, at the LOWEST POSSIBLE PRICES. A visit from the Ladies is solicited, where the prices will be found to be lower than any other House in Town.

Hawking Capes, Cushions, &c. all kinds of Fancy work made up.

NOTE,
21, BURG-STREET, CAPE TOWN.

T. WHITFORD

BEGS to inform his numerous Patrons that, having secured the Services of another experienced ASSISTANT from London, he is enabled to offer Special Advantages. Families and Schools in Town, or anywhere on the Wynberg Line of Rail in the Country, can be waited on at their own Residences.

Arrangements can be made for regular attendance at the Town.

ROYAL HAIR-CUTTING SALOON,
8, Hout-street, Cape Town.

---

8. The front page of the first edition of the *Cape Times*.

CHAPTER NINE

THE OLD SAINT

THE drift of the St. Leger family away from Ireland began in the nineteenth century.

Frederick York St. Leger was born in Limerick on the 20th March, 1833, the third of four surviving sons of Robert, a Heywards Hill St. Leger. While Frederick was still a boy, the family was beset by a string of misfortunes.

The Irish troubles of the 1840s led to the family's removal from Ireland to Monmouthshire, a move which is believed to have caused Frederick's mother, Jane, such chronic homesickness that she slowly wasted away. In 1843, she took her three youngest children on a visit to her father's home in Ballyally, Co. Clare, where she died 'of a broken heart'.

Robert suffered yet another serious setback the same year when, having stood surety for a relative, he was reduced to poverty. Faced with the daunting problem of bringing up four sons and daughter on his own, he moved to London to take up work as a clerk on the P. & O. Shipping Company.

Frederick, now a motherless but clearly a highly intelligent ten year old, was sent to live with his learned uncle, the Rev. William Nassau St. Leger, Vicar of St. Mary-le-Tower in Ipswich. He received his education at St. Paul's School and swathed in an atmosphere of learning he imbibed at an early age an enduring love of the classics. A scholarship saw him to Corpus Christi College, Cambridge, where he was a gold medallist in the Classical Tripos.

His first job – teaching classics at Oundle – did not last long, however. In 1856 he married Christian Emma Muddle, whose father, John Muddle of Shirley, Hampshire, was a purser in the East India Company. The stories he told of the Far East sowed the desire in Frederick York to see far-away places.

The opportunity arrived in the shape of Bishop Gray of Cape Town who visited England in the 1850s to arrange for the creation of two new sees, Grahamstown and Natal, which would divide up his immense diocese into manageable areas. At the same time he cast around for likely candidates to man the new missions; Frederick answered his call. Charged with hope, ideals and dedication, the scholarly young St. Leger sailed away with his wife to the Cape.

Soon after his arrival he was appointed second master at the newly opened St. Andrew's College in the frontier settlement of Grahamstown. His ordination to the Anglican priesthood took place in the recently created Grahamstown Diocese, and promotion to headmaster of the school followed swiftly.

In the face of grave financial difficulties, he managed to build new classrooms with a dormitory and kitchen, and made further improvements to the school at a time when a good education outside Britain was scarcely available and a much coveted prize. Bishop Cotterill reported in 1861 to the first diocesan synod that, 'St. Andrew's boys may now receive an education such as in England can only be obtained in the best grammar schools'.

In 1863 Frederick York became Rector of St. Michael's, Queenstown. His contemporaries did not consider him to be a particularly good preacher. 'He is a clever man,' one of them commented in his diary, 'probably one of the cleverest in the diocese. But I scarcely think he is an orator . . .' Yet on another occasion the same writer heard him preach a really good sermon at the Cathedral which was full of thought expressed in terse, classical English, and concluded that he was indeed a leading man in the diocese.

By 1867, Frederick York had been appointed a canon in the Church and accompanied Bishop Cotterill on a visit to England as his chaplain. His gift to Queenstown when he returned was a set of stained glass windows which now adorn the new St. Michael's Church and are said to be the first stained glass windows to have reached South Africa.

Within a short time Frederick York had established himself as a foremost member of the Church of the Province as well as the father of a large family. He was sent in 1870 to represent the Grahamstown Diocese at its first provincial synod which formulated the constitution of the Church of the Province and was duly appointed secretary of the synod. A potential candidate for the bishopric himself one day, some thought, but in December 1871, he took a curious decision which has puzzled his family ever since.

He resigned his living, clambered on to a wagon with his wife and six children and joined the stampede to the recently opened Kimberley diamond fields. The reason for such a radical change of direction remained Frederick York's secret all his life, though his family still speculate about it in a desultory way.

Possibly the big Colenso controversy concerning the status and jurisdiction of colonial bishoprics which shook the Anglican Church at the time had some influence on him. He could well have been disillusioned with the quarrelling that eroded the Church's credibility. A priest with a family of seven to feed and clothe would need to be absolutely certain of his vocation in a country where members of the clergy were on low stipends and food and clothes prohibitively expensive.

Another possible explanation is suggested by his grandson, Rear-Admiral Malcolm St. Leger Searle, now living in Sussex. 'That his wife became a Roman Catholic was probably the most important factor in his resignation. He was after all *very* Anglican i.e. High Church.'

Yet man is not solely a rational being and Frederick York's action is consistent with many odd decisions taken by St. Legers who have broken away from the routine and ritual of the settled life, like birds escaping from a cage. If there is such a thing as a pattern of irregular behaviour within a family, then Frederick York's decision conforms with it. He is one of those St. Legers who, fairly late in life, awaken to their identities as adventurers. He too, searching for a challenge which would stretch him to his limits, and impelled by a nascent, inchoate desire for that hazy 'something else', risked the journey from the known into the unknown.

The tough fight for survival in the diamond fields was as far removed from life in a rectory as rugby football is from croquet. The family lived rough, Emma sleeping in a primitive shack, the children in tents. The two older boys, Fred and John, did the digging, fruitlessly. Frederick York became a diamond buyer and then attempted newspaper reporting for the *Diamond Field* which he edited in 1873.

Was writing his metier? He suspected it was, so he took his family back to Cape Town over six hundred miles of rough country, covering most of the way by ox wagon. After a short spell as editor of the recently founded *Daily News*, he decided to start up his own newspaper. Until then no one had succeeded in producing a daily newspaper which had lasted in South Africa; Frederick York sensed the time was right for the venture.

The first edition of the *Cape Times*, a modest four-page paper of small format, was published on the 27th March, 1876. That evening in their new home, the family sat together excitedly counting the day's takings, all pennies. Its popularity grew rapidly. The same year the size of the paper was changed to standard newspaper format with the royal coat of arms added to the title, and there it stayed until 1961 when South Africa became a republic.

The paper was the first in the country to make use of the telegraph to gather news, until then carried by mail steamer or post cart.

Frederick York remained in the editorial chair for nearly twenty years achieving the highest possible standards of independent, nineteenth century journalism. The policy to which he adhered faithfully throughout his career was based on his conviction that 'liberty indeed is so far a law of nature to us, individually and nationally, that once the stage of dependence is passed, there can be no moral or political health without it'.[1]

From the outset Frederick York aimed at making the newspaper an honest record of public opinion, 'not the journal of a particular party, but of colonists as a whole'.[2] His editorship spanned one of the most critical periods of South African history, ending in the outbreak of the senseless Boer War.

While Rhodes went about fulfilling his dream of spreading British institutions throughout Africa, Frederick York remained dubious about the methods adopted by Rhodes and the British government to achieve their goal. It was not that Frederick York did not wholeheartedly support colonial expansion. Indeed, he believed as firmly as anyone that Britain offered an almost perfect system of constitutional liberty; his doubts were based on his belief that all methods using force were futile. He saw the Transvaal's victory at Majuba as a healthy setback for the Gladstone government. When the British Prime Minister decided finally to put an end to the Transvaal war and restore the Republic's independence after Britain's sordid annexation of the territory, the *Cape Times* commented:

> 'There is nothing in this unhappy story, now we trust closed, to hinder us from working together for the welfare of our adopted land, or from building up in concert a community which will one day hope to have traditions of its own worthy of a place in history.'[3]

While Frederick York openly admired Rhodes, 'with all my criticisms of Rhodes' policy, I have still retained an affection for his personality', he was sceptical about Rhodes accepting the premiership of Cape Colony whilst retaining his position as Chairman of the Chartered Company and of the British South Africa Company. The paper took the view that a conflict of interest would be inevitable at some future date, a judgement vindicated by the Jameson Raid in 1895, that ill-starred sally engineered by Rhodes into the Boer-inhabited Transvaal. The British defeat at the hands of the Boers brought Rhodes down and added coals to a fire ultimately to flare up as the Boer War.

Through the period of his editorship Frederick York pleaded for the application of consideration and justice in all Britain's dealings with the Boers and the tribal African peoples the British government desired theoretically to protect. The paper was vocal in local affairs too, giving sufficient space to the citizens of the colony to air their grievances.

In 1895, Frederick York relinquished his editorship though he did retain sole control over the editorial management in his lifetime. He had worked untiringly for nearly twenty years to build up the paper.

G. A. L. Green, a reporter on the *Cape Times* in the 1890s and later to become a prominent editor himself of the *Cape Argus*, admitted that at the time of Frederick York's retirement he wielded, 'absolute and exclusive control of the newspaper which his transparent honesty, incessant hard work, and sound judgement had made easily the greatest organ of opinion in South Africa'.[4] Without doubt, Frederick

York was considered by his contemporaries to be the greatest journalist of his time. Green thought him to be 'perhaps the most polished writer who has ever supplied regular copy to the press of South Africa. But certain it is that his articles were widely read and admired by all classes.'[5] His scholarship and his phenomenal memory for people, places and politics, linked with his wide experience of the human condition had equipped him well for his late vocation.

Cape Town dubbed him 'the Old Saint'. A familiar figure in the streets of the city, he was always sartorially clad in a top hap and spats and never forgot his cane. Making friends did not come easily to him and he remained aloof, though his association with the distinguished politician James Rose Innes was lifelong. Some interpreted his natural reserve as 'uppishness', a notion repudiated by Green who knew him to be a very shy person, yet 'free from intellectual arrogance'. His family remember him as a soft-spoken, gentle, kindly person who doted on his grandchildren. His generosity extended to receiving a dead half-brother's son into his family and educating him.

Immediately following his retirement, Frederick York took a more active part in public affairs, becoming a town councillor in 1895. He stood for election to the Upper House of the Cape Parliament but was defeated, an event he attributed to Rhodes's personal opposition to him. But the people were not to be thwarted: very soon afterwards he was returned for Cape Town with the highest number of votes, to the Legislative Assembly, the Cape's Lower House.

Any political career he might have planned for himself was however cut short by a serious throat complaint. On a visit to England a specialist diagnosed cancer. Back in Cape Town he underwent a tracheotomy and two further operations — to no avail. He died at his home in Newlands on the 28th March, 1901, and was buried in Camp Ground Cemetery of St. Thomas's Church, Rondebosch.[6]

In his minutely-researched account of those early days of the *Cape Times,* Gerald Shaw records in *Some Beginnings* that at the Old Saint's funeral, 'the great and the famous of the Peninsula were present including Sir Gordon Sprigg, again Prime Minister of the Cape, W.P. Schreiner, members of the Cabinet, the bench and the leaders of commerce and the professions in the Peninsula'.[7] T. L. Graham, the

Colonial Secretary, and fellow-directors of the *Cape Times* were amongst the pallbearers.

His death was universally mourned. The *Midland News* praised his qualities in an editorial of March 29th, 1901.

> 'The late Mr. St. Leger raised the Cape Times to the position of the leading paper in the country and whilst under his personal control that paper was a safe guide to the peaceful development of South Africa. When his health began to fail, he retired from active service on the paper, but still took a keen interest in the affairs of the country. Possessed of a true patriotism, a sound judgement, clear perception of the trend of various forces working in South Africa and a facile pen, he did much to shape its destinies; and our regret is that through failing health the influence of his guiding hand was lost during recent critical years . . . South Africa has lost one of its truest patriots.'

But it was Edmund Garrett who had taken over as editor after Frederick York retired who paid the 'Old Saint' perhaps the most eloquent tribute of all.

> 'This is not the place to dwell on his political teachings — a high-minded Imperialism with a strong vein of Christian socialism . . . But of his public work let me say this; not a newspaper writer among us but is the better for it, the better able to rise above all that is tawdry, or servile or unchivalrous. It means much for the broadening river of South African journalism that it flowed near the source with so pure a stream.'[8]

BALLADS FROM "PUNCH"

AND OTHER POEMS

BY

WARHAM ST. LEGER

LONDON
DAVID STOTT, 370, OXFORD STREET, W
1890

9. Title page of Ballads from 'Punch' by Warham St. Leger.

CHAPTER TEN

NINE CENTURIES ON

THE following generation produced a crop of aspiring writers though Frederick York is best remembered. He had spent his boyhood at the vicarage in Ipswich in the company not only of his uncle and aunt but also with his six cousins, Rupert, Warham, Hugh, William, Arthur and Marion.

The premature death of the Rev. William Nassau St. Leger in 1861 left his wife almost penniless — in the way of clergy widows then.

Her sons were educated at the Clergy Orphan School, Canterbury. Rupert and Warham got themselves to Cambridge, Rupert as a Greek scholar. Eventually he took Orders and finally drifted into a living in Cornwall and a Grecian world of his own. At heart he was a poet, writing verse in a desultory way. His children were christened with ancient, evocative Celtic names.

William too turned to the pen for his leisure though he also had considerable musical talent. He left England for India, settled in Madras, edited the *Madras Mail* and became organist in Madras Cathedral. His son Frank studied music and later on accompanied Melba on her tours as her accompanist.

Whether Arthur wrote, no-one knows; for some unexplained reason he was packed off to a far-flung destination and never heard of again; the Victorians kept loyally mum about the mystery of Arthur's disappearance.

Hugh was quite different from his more scholarly brothers. Not for him the cloistered life of the university. He spurned education, finally running away to sea in search of adventure. Later on in life he joined the army, travelling with his wife to the farthest outposts of the British Empire. When at last they returned to England, Hugh began writing boys' adventure stories, action-packed tales of heroes who embodied all the virtues and desirable characteristics of brave and gallant Englishmen of the Victorian period.

His stories are permeated with the ethos of the age. One of them, *Skeleton Reef*, tells of Jack Rollock, an archetypal decent, courageous English boy with a longing for the sea in his veins. Hugh must have easily identified himself with his hero since the description of Jack contains as much truth as fantasy:

> 'Jack Rollock was the only son of a naval officer, who had been killed during an encounter with a slave dhow whilst he was still a baby. Consequently his mother had lavished all her affection on him. She was never tired of telling him long yarns about sea fights and foreign lands which she had heard from her husband. These tales young Jack listened to with keenest interest and inwardly determined to follow the profession of his father though he never mentioned this resolve to his mother, as he knew it would pain her; and she, poor lady, continued to tell him tales which fired his blood, in happy ignorance of the effect they had upon him.'[1]

Jack's perilous adventures take place in the South Seas, a scene as evocative of mystery and fascination for the Victorian boy as outer space is to the modern child. He copes with the kind of hazards secretly yearned for by a Victorian schoolboy, running away from school to sea and adrift for days on end on the open ocean, cut off from civilization, eventually to be picked up by an illicitly-run slave ship. By his efforts alone two slaves are released and together they escape to discover a new South Sea island which, in true British fashion, Jack names after himself. The island is colonized by people from a neighbouring island — for their own good.

The dream of being a Cecil Rhodes of the South Seas, dedicated to spreading English culture, trade and Christianity would have excited a boy of the last century: no-one had yet seriously challenged the validity of such aspirations. The books Hugh wrote are deeply religious, an ideal choice for Sunday school prizes then. They are tales of a world which is in order wherever the British are present and where good always triumphs over evil.

The first book, an immediate success, was followed up by several more, all of them popular, a gratifying reward for someone so unambitious for fame or fortune. In his stories Hugh was able to recall experiences of his young sea-faring days; they reflect his ever youthful, innocent personality. He is an archetypal St. Leger in many respects. Mrs. Eigen Ramsay Murray, his daughter, could be describing so many St. Legers when she says of her father:

> 'Unfailingly kind and tolerant, amusing as were all St. Legers, but unwordly-wise in assuming that all with whom he had business dealings were as honest as himself. He was a devout churchman.'[2]

St. Leger humour ran strongest through brilliant, shy Warham who possessed a beguiling charm to boot. For a time on the staff of *Punch*, he enjoyed a brief spell in the literary limelight, but not one to pursue his opportunities — like most St. Legers — drifted out of the public eye into a more effortless way of life. He enjoyed writing for its own sake. One of his jauntiest works is the libretto for *Cigarette*, a light, romantic opera first performed in Cardiff in 1892. But his best legacy is his comic verse. Over a hundred of his ballads and poems were published in 1890 in a volume entitled *Ballads from Punch and Other Poems*, excellent examples of the type of humour likely to keep late nineteenth century *Punch* readers amused. They express a typical St. Leger slant on life, yet the themes, The Boat Race, Parliament, The Derby, love . . . are perennial subjects for the humorist of any age. Even Ireland is as much in the news as it ever was.

A CRY FROM DUBLIN

If ye seek for the cause of the present disthress,
And look for a way to get out of the mess,
To free poor ould Ireland from throuble and fear,
Ye've only to give us a Parliament here.

There's a somethin' the Government can't understand.
We don't care for rint, and we don't care for land;
We've a heap of respect for the Queen on her throne,
But we do want a Parliament-house of our own.

Sure, the bhoy wid a turn for display'd have a chance
Of takin' the flure of the House for a dance;
Or gettin' its ear – in his teeth – by-and-bye,
Or catchin' the Spaker a one in the eye.

I can see how 'twould be on a field-night so gay,
Wid the ladies upsthairs to encourage the play,
While the Spaker steps out in the iligant scene,
Wid the mace round his head and his wig on the green.

Oh! Ireland, me counthry, what glory and fun
When the struggle is over, the Parliament won!
A happier counthry will never be known
When we manage affairs in a way of our own.

A BOAT-RACE BALLAD

Of all the signs that make it clear
   That England's power is going
There's naught so sad as what we hear,
In gloomy chorus year by year,
   About the art of rowing.

Or can it be that critics use
   Imagination's quiver
For random shots against the crews
Who represent the rival blues
   Each year upon the river?

They feather high, they feather low,
   They do not swing together;
The wonder is the boat can go
When those who pull can neither row,
   Nor swing, nor slide, nor feather

They're late and early, short and long;
   They miss the stroke's beginning;
They do, in fact, so much that's wrong
That neither crew, however strong,
   Seems capable of winning.

AN EQUINE SOLILOQUY

The Derby Day — a perfect day — bright sun and lively breeze,
And e'en the bridge at Charing Cross looks pretty through the trees;
Or it may be — for what am I? — a broken-down old hoss —
The trees look pretty 'cause they hide the bridge at Charing Cross.

The cab rank's quiet and empty — the best have gone away,
A festive crowd to Epsom town this merry Derby Day;
But I — the growler's shafts a world too wide for my shrunk flank —
With drooping head and shaky legs, remain upon the rank.

You'd hardly think, to look at me, that some few years ago
I faced the flag on Derby Day — twelve thoroughbreds a-row;
Crack tipsters said they never saw a better-looking horse,
And no-one now in London town will drive me to the course.

Yes, I was famous once, and lived! And now I've naught to tell
But endless drives from Euston Square to dreary Camberwell;
And while they pile big boxes up I wish that I were dead.
Or grudge a sixpence in the fare – and I a thoroughbred!

The cab-yard cannot kill the joy that swells the racer's heart —
I see the scene in fancy's eye, it's getting near the start.
I see the Beauties in their pride; oh how that pride 'twould stab
To hint that they may come, like me, to draw a four-wheeled cab.

Oh! might I find my weary hoofs once more upon the sward
Before I limp that last sad morn into the knacker's yard,
Oh! might I leave the sombre skies and sooty air of town,
And snuff the living speed that streams across the breezy down.

Then for a while I know I'd leave my ills behind,
And race in mad delight abreast of any wind;
Fly o'er the rhythmic-beaten turf, and mock the swallows skimming —
'Four-wheeler!' 'Right, mum. Here you are.
Kim up!' All right. I'm kimming.

A SUMMER SOLILOQUY
By Jacques Junior

A bee, or not a bee? That is the question.
Whether 'twere better not to mind, and suffer
The stings that every summer are our portion,
Or take the trouble but to move an arm,
And, by opposing, end them. It flies — it creeps,
It creeps, perchance it stings! Then comes the rub,
When we have shuffled off our clothing. Soft,
'Twas but a bluebottle! How sweet it is
To lie like this i' the sun, and think of nought;
And that meseems to many wordy sages
Were small refreshment in this windy time.
How many are there who do cheat themselves,
And with themselves the many, that they are
The very vaward leaders of the fray,
The lictors of pomp of intellect.
Whereas they are the merest driven spray,
The running rabble heralding the march
Impelled by what they herald; —
Who ever glance behind to see which way —
Oh, my prophetick soul! my Aunt Eliza!
            (He is stung!)

ON THE RECEIPT OF A PHOTOGRAPH

And is my hair as thin as that,
    And are my feet so big,
And am I really getting fat,
    With eyes like slumbrous pig?
And does the smile, wherewith I thought
    To show the peace within,
Appear with wreathed folly fraught
    Like this insensate grin.

Small wonder when, amid the dance,
    I seek the young and fair,

They ask, with soft, confiding glance,
   'Oh, *would* you mind a square?'
While rage and wounded vanity,
   Like mingled powders fizz,
I cry, 'Is this dark daub like me?'
   And conscience cries, 'It is!'

Ah! like the splash that makes you mad,
   And Amaryllis scream,
When in swift launch the careless cad
   Goes hurling up the stream,
Or when the cloudland crystals fleck
   The air with feathery mazes
A snowball bursts upon your neck
   And makes you jump like blazes

Or when the booby trap is sprung
   Above your chamber door,
Or when the chairless weight is flung,
   Unchecked upon the floor
Or like the street door's sudden slam,
   Such is the shock to me,
Contrasting what I really am
   With what I hoped to be.

Farewell the dreams of fond romance,
   Of wedding bells and dresses,
The dear discomforts of the dance,
The fancied fondness of a glance,
   False smiles and doubtful tresses.
Henceforth I spurn the worldling-crew,
   Renounce my cousin Mabel,
And yield myself heart-whole unto
   The pleasures of the table.

A BALLAD OF SALAD

I cannot eat the red, red rose,
   I cannot eat the white;

In vain the long laburnum glows,
Vain the camellia's waxen snows,
  The lily's cream of light

The lilac's clustered chalices
  Proffer their bounty sweet
In vain! Though very good for bees,
Man with unstinted yearning sees,
  Admires, but cannot eat.

Give me the lettuce that has cool'd
  Its heart in the rich earth,
Till every joyous leaf is school'd
  To crisply-crinkled mirth;

Give me the mustard and the cress,
  Whose glistening stalklets stand
As silver-white as nymphs by night
  Upon the moonlit strand;

The winking radish, round and red,
  That like a ruby shines;
And the faint blessing, onion shred,
  Whene'er Lucullus dined.

The wayward endive's curling head,
  Cool cucumber sliced small,
And let the imperial beetroot spread
  Her purple over all.

Though shrinking poets still prefer
  The common floral fashions,
With buds and blossoms hymn their Her,
These vegetable loves would stir
  A flint-heart's mineral passions.

A SEASONABLE DITTY

A month ago I had a cold,
  And when my family I told,

Nine Centuries On

They all exclaimed, 'Oh, rubbish!'
And all the solace that I got
Consisted in a treatment hot,
   Hot-groggy and hot-tubbish.

My symptoms met with jeer and scoff;
They heard unmoved my plaintive cough,
   And told me, void of pity,
Instead of staying warm at home,
'Twould do me far more good to roam
   As usual to the City.

The self-same symptoms — only slight —
Are radiant with the lurid light
   Of the new epidemic,
And now that Turnham Green is 'down',
They swathe me in my dressing gown,
   And proffer potions chemick.

Obedient to affections's call,
To depths of huskiness I fall,
   In tremulous cadenza;
What though a native cold they jeer,
They treat with mix'd respect and fear,
   A Russian Influenza.

A while ago, without remorse,
A slighter cold would mean divorce
   A toro nec non mensa;
But the whole household now hangs round
Conciliated by the sound
   Of Russian Influenza.

'Twould hurt their feelings should I say
A word of going out today;
   So, free from business trammels,
To peaceful eve from cosy morn
I will the study walls adorn
   With Aspinall's enamels.

Though sweet these restful moments are,
In years to come the light catarrh
  Will sigh 'Che farò senza
Those tender cares that lent a charm
To all the sudden wild alarm
  Of Russian Influenza?'

A SUMMER BUZZING

Busy, curious, thirsty fly,
Who's to drink it, you or I?
For you follow every sip
With persistence to the lip,
Or each vain endeavour close
With a buzz about my nose,
Or frustrate it by surprise
Darting at my blinking eyes,
Till despairingly I cry,
'O confound this thirsty fly!'

Nay, art gone? Thy pardon — There!
Now I feel you on my hair,
Now a sudden hum I hear
Menacing the shrinking ear.
Come, stern measures I must try
To expunge this curious fly.

True, for both of us there's room
In creation — where's the broom?
True, thy little life to thee
Is as much as mine to me;
True, that thy intelligence;
Is for they small size immense;
But believe 'twas madness quite
To molest me thus tonight.

There I have thee, on the floor
Slipper stills thee evermore!
So thy little life past,

Safe from scorching wick at last,
Safe from ruthless spider's net,
Safe from boys more cruel yet —

Out of danger, out of pain,
Thou wilt never buzz again!
Vase of azure glass, I wis,
Whence thy name derivèd is,
Shall piece its shattered ere
Thou again my cup wilt share.
Though the floor be somewhat mess'd,
Still whatever is is best;
So no more my patience try,
Busy, curious, thirsty fly.

WORDS FOR MUSIC

The singer's voice was tender,
   Her eyes were large and bright,
She fix'd her gaze upon him
   And sang with all her might.
I know not what she was singing,
   Nor why she looked his way;
But there suddenly came upon him
   A feeling of dismay.

For he saw that the space around him
   Had larger and larger grown,
Where the lustrous eyes had found him,
   And fastened him there — alone
And myriad eyes that he could not see
   With anguish made him sweat,
From the china-blue of the soldier blonde
   To the brown of the pert brunette.

And he felt that his nose was swelling,
   And he knew that his face was red,
And the bald, bald spot seemed spreading
   Till it covered his shrinking head.

And he knew that his coat sat badly,
  And his shoes waxed suddenly tight,
And he thought that his tie was very awry,
  And he trembled to put it right.

But the singer his soul was sounding,
  As she caroll'd of passion and pain,
And he vowed in a whirl of surging thought
  That he'd never come there again.
And time in infinite circles
  Seemed spreading and spreading round,
Where Fate, like a pebble had dropped him there,
  In an ocean of pain profound.

And the tune in his ears was ringing
  As he stumbled against the door,
And he cannon'd against a waiter,
  And the coffee ran over the floor.
And he tried to tip the Vicar,
  And trod on the Persian cat,
And he hurried away with a stranger's coat
  And someone's else's hat.

THE PLAINT OF THE GRAND PIANO

I was a grand piano once — nay, hearken what I say —
The grandeur is no longer here, it left me yesterday.
One leather-souled executant at a sitting could demolish
The mellow pride of tuneful years, of tone, and power, and polish.

A dapper man, with weary brow, and smile of conscious pow'r,
A Jove, prepared to improvise tone-thunder by the hour
Is Nasmyth Hammermann, whose touch would disconcert the dead,
Whose foot would rush with pedal-crush where angels fear to tread.

He kept his soul in patience while lesser people played,
As one who bears with cruder views that taste-bound souls degrade;
He pitied plaintive melody and winning modulation,
Biding his time — and then it came — the afternoon's sensation.

He hovered over the keyboard, like a wild beast over its prey,
And he tossed his head, and he rattled his wrists — and then he began
to play;
To play! And in that crowded room was none with heart to see
That what was play to him and them was worse than death to me!

He struck a chord, as a hawk strikes a lark who is dumb with fear,
And his fingers spread over the octaves like a slander in full career,
And my overstrung nerves that waited the worst nigh sprung from the
shuddering case
As he finished his horrible prelude with an awful bang in the base

He gloated; I waited; and then began a butchery great and grim,
And melody screamed and harmony writhed, and form, rent limb
from limb,
Was hurled in murdrous Largesse to the careless, ravening crowd
Who chatted and laugh'd the louder, as my agony waxed more loud.

He checked his course, and he wriggled round, till he found the soul
of pain,
And he thumped it with pitiless finger, again, again, again!
Then, like a pawing horse let go, he tore at headlong pace,
And drowned the tortured treble's cry in the roar of an anguished bass.

My tenderest tones, that answer clear the artist's lightest touch,
Were yank'd in handfuls out like hair in some fierce maniac's clutch,
And my beautiful keys, that never yet had sullied their tuneful pride,
Like elephants with the tusk-ache in ivory anguish cried.

Hark to the murmurs sad and low, self-struck upon my strings,
Such music as a dying love, unknown, unsolaced sings,
For yesterday's undreamt disgrace can never not have been,
And I must shrink from music now, and sob 'Unclean, unclean!'

The girls have practised on me in endless ladders of scales,
Whereby they mounted to castled heights, and the realms of fairy
tales;
And I loved their wayward endeavours, and my patient sweetness at
last

Won them to tell me their love's young dreams as I hallowed their
                                                  childhood's past.
And the Governess, meek and modest, who counted the tale of bars,
Would slip from the sleeping children, and the school-room worries
                                                         and jars;
And the tender heart would open to me, and, work-a-day woes forgot,
The pencil-cramped hands would tremble, and the tears from her heart
                                                       well'd hot.

They called her a Perfect Treasure, but 'twas I alone who knew
They tale of the young life's struggle, so tender and brave and true;
And when she touched me I told it, and somebody listened and
                                                       learned,
And the winter-time went out of her life, and the daffodil days
returned.

And Maud in her tempers would bang away — Sweet Maud — for I
                                                      often heard
The fortissimo suddenly ended in a kiss like the chirp of a bird
And Mabel's curious reveries — how soon a piano discovers
When a girl gives one hand to her music, and the other is clasped in her
                                                         lover's.

Perchance some tender hand again may soothe my tortured heart,
May heal the scars of Hammermann with balm of rare Mozart;
Perchance the Nocturne's mystic feet may through my caverns stray,
When great Beethoven's passion-storms have cleansed the plague
                                                          away.

But no, farewell that happy past; henceforth I'm only fit
To play the concertina's part to wandering niggers' wit;
Or, as a street piano, find as jubilant a goal
As a wet day in China when you do not know a soul.

Yet it may be my past deserts may win a loftier place,
Low in the outer walks of Art, not blatant in disgrace;
And music's tutelary powers may bid their Outcast go
And be the sacred music in a panoramic show,
And moan 'The Village Blacksmith' when the lights are burning low.

PRAENUNTIA VERIS

A token from the coming Spring
  Has greeted me today,
Which tears into my eyes can bring,
  And stop me on my way.

'Tis not that in the pathway lies
  A primrose heedless tost;
'Tis not the martyr bud which dies
  Before the lingering frost.

Nor yet the subtle whisper, heard
  Clear 'mid the blustering wind,
That tells of flower, and bee, and bird,
  And April days behind.

No! 'twas that while with eager pace
  Heedless I hurried by,
A gnat, the firstling of the race,
  Flew straight into my eye!

10. Sir Thomas St. Leger and Anne (Plantagenet).

CHAPTER ELEVEN

THE RIGHT TO ARMS

SINCE the death of the last Viscount Doneraile and Frederick York's generation, the bearing of arms has become less fashionable. Nevertheless, many members of ancient families frequently ask, 'have I the right to bear arms?'

In an age where people have been reduced to mere numbers on cards destined for computer processing, the interest in heraldry is on the increase. The displaying of arms on carriages, silver or stationery is seldom seen nowadays and misconceptions have grown around the practice.

In heraldic law there is so no such thing as a coat of arms for a surname. One is entitled to arms if descent can be proved from a male in the family who is on official record as being entitled to arms. Even when arms appear on monuments or tombs of ancestors, the right to arms is not proved. An Officer of the College of Arms, — whose duty it once was to proclaim war but today is mainly occupied by tracing genealogies and superintending state ceremonies — can only certify a person as armigerous if that person's right is on record in the official registers of the College.

Originally these records were made after a Herald from the College had made a tour of the country towns and seats of families to ascertain and record genealogies and the right to bear arms of the nobility and gentry of England. Such Visitations were undertaken primarily for tax purposes.

Sir Robert St. Leger's name appears on the Roll of Norman knights in St. Mary's Church, Battle, though no arms are recorded. The so-called Battle Abbey Roll is a fictitious roll for which no original ever existed. There are 16th- and 17th-century Herald's copies among the manuscripts at the British Library, none of them including arms. No-one has traced the hereditary use of Coats of Arms earlier than the second quarter of the 12th century.

The St. Leger family's arms, *Azure fretty Argent a Chief Or*, appear in parish churches all over Kent — Sir Anthony's arms can be seen represented twice in the Great Cloister Vault of Canterbury Cathedral. In his mammoth study of Kent, Edward Hasted notes that Sir John St. Leger, Sheriff of Kent in Henry VI's reign, was returned in a list drawn up in the twelfth year of Henry's kingship as one of the county's gentlemen who had the right to bear the coat armour of his ancestors.

The earliest representation of the arms outside Kent appears above the brass of Sir Thomas and Anne St. Leger in St. George's Chapel, Windsor. The arms were first put on official record after the Herald's Visitations of Devon in 1531 when they were allowed to the family at Annery. Sir John's family was allowed supporters, on the dexter *a Falcon Argent armed Or* and on the sinister *a Griffin passant per bend sinister Or fretty Azure and Or*.

Since this branch of the family has long since expired so have the arms. A griffin passant can be seen on the left above the head of Ralph as he is depicted on the brass in Ulcombe Church. While no arms are represented it seems probable that the griffin is the most ancient distinguishing emblem of the family. The Heywards Hill branch is stiff with griffins; they form the crest and supporters of their arms. The origin of the family motto, *Haut et Bon*, is not traceable in English records.

When John Chester assumed the surname and arms of St. Leger by Royal Licence of 1863, they were quartered with his own paternal arms: *Azure fretty Argent a Chief Or thereon for distinction a Cross Crosslet Azure quartered with Ermine two chevrons Azure*.

The College of Arms houses innumerable ancient documents amounting to an enormous deposit of English history. Anyone interested in family history may apply to the Officers at the College who will undertake a search on his behalf.

EPILOGUE

A few St. Legers live on. The twentieth century opened up more opportunities than ever before for the expression of talent. Liberated for good from the orthodoxy and class taboos which still governed the choice of career for latter-day gentry even as late as the 1930s, St. Legers were able to choose any way of life they felt inclined to follow. Sir Robert's descendants today have careers in art, medicine, teaching, architecture and aviation to mention a few; not many ever chose commerce. Yet however diverse their professions their children are all destined to share the common experience of having to parry questions about whether they have closed the stable door or if they enjoy their oats.

Would Sir Robert recognize them? In an age when they no longer share a similar kind of existence imposed by land tenure and its attendant responsibilities, the question inevitably arises as to whether they have any habits or features in common which make them recognizable as St. Legers. The family would say yes: heavy eyebrows and humour. Incredibly, even a joke cracked by Anthony in the sixteenth century was recorded by one of his contemporaries. Neither does humour seem to be restricted to the English side of the family; a Thévenin de St. Léger was jester at the Court of Charles V of France.

At any gathering nowadays with a St. Leger present, he is the quiet man with the straight face and the raised eyebrow who is flanked by people clutching their bellies in mirth. The only example which springs immediately to the present writer's mind is the occasion when her brother arrived home after a cycle tour with his arm in plaster of Paris.

'Oh God, what will Mummy say?' the horrified sister cried. 'Who knows,' replied the remarkably calm young man through pursed lips, 'but just wait till she sees this,' and smiling engagingly, he revealed the gap left by the tooth he had lost in the same accident.

Their natural habitat is the country. If a St. Leger lives from necessity in town, he is dreaming of his country cottage and a garden to tend. This is not to say a town-loving St. Leger with delicate eyebrows is not pure stock; he (or she) is merely an exception to the rule. A quiet gardening life is far more preferable to the clan than the superficial social round. Quiet and unassuming, they like to merge with their landscape. Centuries of a rural existence are not easily shaken off; the English countryside always tugged at its legitimate offspring.

Even if Sir Robert failed to recognise the world in which they live, he might know them by these features, and one more — a constant, nine centuries old; a rather old-fashioned, unwavering loyalty to their monarch.

APPENDIX ONE
Knights and Sheriffs
Knights of Kent

Sir Ralph St. Leger	appointed 1347
Sir Ralph St. Leger	appointed 1386

Sheriffs of Kent

Sir Ralph St. Leger	1386-7
Sir Thomas St. Leger	1397
Sir William St. Leger	1408
Sir John St. Leger	1431
Ralph St. Leger	1468
Sir Ralph St. Leger	1503
Sir Anthony St. Leger	1539
Sir Warham St. Leger	1559

Sheriff of Surrey

Sir Thomas St. Leger	1470

Sheriffs of Devon

Sir George St. Leger	1531
Sir John St. Leger	1560

APPENDIX TWO

Members of Parliament

Sir Ralph St. Leger }	present at the Great Council as representatives for Kent in 1254.	
Sir Hugh St. Leger }		
Sir Ralph St. Leger	Kent	1344
		1346
		1351
Sir Arnald	Kent	1376-7
Sir Ralph	Kent	1379 (Chancellor in 2nd Parliament
	Essex	1384 of Richard II)
Sir John	Romney (a cinque port)	1449
Sir John	Dartmouth	1555
	Devon	1559
	Arundel	1562-3
	Devon	1571
	Devon	1572
	Tregony	1584
Sir Anthony	Kent	1559
Nicolas	Maidstone	1571
		1572
Major General Anthony	Great Grimsby	1768-74
John Hayes	Okehampton	1790

House of Lords

Hayes St. Leger, 3rd Viscount Doneraile	1830-1854
Hayes St. Leger, 4th Viscount Doneraile	1855-1887

APPENDIX THREE

Manors and Lands in Kent held by St. Legers at Various Periods between the 11th and 18th Centuries

Bilsington Manor, Priory and lands — Newchurch Hundred
Belgrave Manor
Brookes, Higham — Shamel Hundred
Bace (Bays Farm) Ickham — Downhamford Hundred
Barton Manor — Wingham Hundred
Bromfield Rectory and lands — Eyhorne Hundred
Bilsington House and all lands of Tonge
Chantry Farm, Hedcorne — Eyhorne Hundred
Coninbrooke Manor (Kennington) — Longbridge Hundred
Chequer — Wingham Hundred
Chiltern Manor — Wingham Hundred
Ellenden Manor, parish of Seasalter
Elnothington Manor — Eyhorne Hundred
Eversley Manor — Calehill Hundred
Greenway Court — Eyhorne Hundred
Harbilton Manor — Eyhorne Hundred
Harrietsham Manor — Eyhorne Hundred
Heyton Manor — Stowting Hundred
Leeds Castle — Eyhorne Hundred
Leeds Priory, House and site and houses and lands
Langley Manor — Eyhorne Hundred
Lenham Manor — Eyhorne Hundred
Lenham Rectory — Eyhorne Hundred
Molland Manor — Wingham Hundred
Murley Court Manor — Eyhorne Hundred
Newbarne Lees (Dudmanswike) Langport Hundred
Okington Manor
Pising Manor[1]
Pising Manor[2] — Cornilo Hundred
Pen Court Manor, Hollingbourne — Eyhorne Hundred
Selling Rectory and Parsonage — Boughton Hundred
Sutton Valence — Eyhorne Hundred

Ulcombe Manor — Eyhorne Hundred
Wilmington Manor, Boughton Aluph — Wye Hundred
Wierton House — Boughton — Eyhorne Hundred
West Farborn Manor — Eyhorne Hundred
Woodnesborough Manor — Eastry Hundred

APPENDIX FOUR

Two 16th-century letters

(Above) Letter from Sir Walter Raleigh to Lord Leicester. Dated Leismore, August 1581. (Overleaf) Letter from Sir Warham St. Leger to Lord Burghley, July 1571.

APPENDIX FIVE

(Author's note: From the beginning of my research I was aware of the presence of St. Legers in France, but decided that extending my investigations to include them would be too daunting a task. The typescript of this book was already being prepared for publication when Maurice Baron de Saint Leger, head of the family in France, told me the amazing story of his family history and provided me with copy of an unbroken genealogical chart going back to 1030. To have omitted this information altogether would have been grossly negligent, and the following provides a brief summary of this important branch of the family's history.)

The Saint Legers of the County of Kilkenny

by the Baron de St. Leger

There was a branch of the house of St. Leger settled in Ireland at a remote period, and its founder, William de Saint Leger, was a great-great-grandson of Robert de Saint Leger who fought at Hastings in 1066.

William, who held the Castle of Carmarthen in Wales (1185-1200), was a man trusted by William le Marechal, Earl of Pembroke, as his well-beloved and faithful knight. (See Register of St. Thomas's Abbey, Dublin). He went to Ireland with Le Marechal in 1192, and was invested with large estates in the counties of Kilkenny, Leix and also Westmeath, by King John. He was Lord of the Manors of Rosconnel and Tullaghanbrogue near the town of Kilkenny, where the St. Legers had connections until the end of the 17th century. He had several sons, of whom William succeeded him to the Kilkenny fiefs, and Peter received the Westmeath possessions. Peter's descendants enjoyed prosperity: there were two Bishops of Meath amongst them – Thomas de Saint Leger (1286-1320) and William de Saint Leger (1350-2). This branch of the Westmeath St. Legers suffered greatly, owing to Robert Bruce's invasion of Ireland (1315-17).

William, eldest son of William (this Christian name runs from father to eldest sons until the middle of the 14th century) held father to eldest sons until the middle of the 14th century) held Rosconnel and Tullaghanbrogue in 1247, and his son Geoffrey was Bishop of Ossory (1260-86) – 'the second founder of the Cathedral of St. Canice' – while another William was Bishop of Leighlin and died at the Papal Court of Avignon in 1348.

The fourth William of the line was summoned to Parliament as a baron in 1310, and was Seneschal of the Liberty of Kilkenny (1311-14) in which office he was wounded, fighting the Irish rebels.

In 1306 the fifth William married Joan Purcel, heiress to the Barony of Obargy, otherwise Slewmargy in Leix and Carlow, and the title of Baron of Slewmargy then passed to each head of the family.

Thomas de Saint Leger, grandson of the fifth William was raised to the peerage in 1382 – but he had no son, rendering this first Irish St. Leger peerage extinct.

John de Saint Leger, younger son of the fifth William, also fought against Irish rebels. In 1359 King Edward III ordered 'our well-beloved valet John de Saint Leger to be paid for the services of himself with another man at arms 12d per day and eighteen *hobillars* at 4d per day, in the suite of Amalric de St. Amand and against the O'Mores of Slewmargy'. In 1362 he held the town of Leighlin against the MacMurroughs and O'Ryans.

John fitz John de Saint Leger, his son, was *custos pacis* of Kilkenny in the following reign, and Sheriff of the Cross of Kilkenny (1395-1404). The office of shrievalty of the Liberty of Kilkenny was frequently held by members of the St. Leger family during the following two centuries. (*History of St. Canice's Cathedral*, Prim and Graves, 1856)

In the second part of the 15th century, the head of the house was Patrick Saint Leger of Tullaghanbrogue, styled 'Chief of his Nation', and great-grandson of John fitz John. In 1491 he went on a pilgrimage to St. James of Compostella and Jerusalem, and in 1495 he witnessed the will of Sir James Butler, probably a dear relative. He died in 1498 leaving two sons, Edmund and William.

William, the younger son, was the founder of the Ballyfennon branch, otherwise Newtown, which flourished in the 16th and 17th centuries but was extinct by the middle of the 18th century.

Appendix Five

Edmund Saint Leger of Tullaghanbrogue, 'Captain of his Nation', was in conflict with the Friars Preachers and Minors of Kilkenny, because he disputed gifts made to convents by his ancestors. A sentence of excommunication was directed against him by the Bishop of Ossory (1509). (*Irish Monastic and Episcopal Deeds*, Newport B. White, 1936).

His son, Oliver Saint Leger, 'Lord of Tullaghanbrogue and Baron of Rosconnel', was elected Sovereign of Kilkenny in 1533. In 1537 'Lord Slygger and Jamys Slygger (of Ballyfennon)' were found guilty by the verdict of the Corporation of the town of Kilkenny for 'they doo use at their pleasure to chargue their tenauntes and all the kinges subjectes within the said countie with Coyn and Livery'.

Patrick, his son and heir, was styled the Baron St. Leger, 'alias the Baron Lyster'. In April 1550 the Lord of Upper Ossory 'accompagnied by divers evil disposed persons ... with force and arms ...' invaded the manor of Rosconnel, expelling 'the St. Legers tenants etc.'. The law suit *Saint Leger v. Upper Ossory* was rendered in favour of Patrick Saint Leger, owing to the help of Sir Anthony St. Leger, then Viceroy in Ireland and Patrick's distant relative.

Sir George Saint Leger of Tullaghanbrogue, great-grandson of this Patrick, together with his cousin, Father William Saint Leger, a Jesuit, took part in the rising of 1641 which is known by the name of the 'Confederation of Kilkenny'. George was a Representative in the Parliament of the General Assembly in 1644, and also a member of the government of the Province of Leinster. His cousin William, a learned theologian and agent to the Papal Nuncio, Cardinal Rinuccini, afterwards became a fierce opponent to the Cardinal, for he supported peace with King Charles while the Nuncio wanted to continue the war. Sir George Saint Leger and his eldest son Patrick were attainted by the Cromwellian regime in 1653, and submitted a claim for restoration to Charles II in 1666. The Saint Legers were again attainted as Stuart supporters by William III in 1691 and 1696.

John Saint Leger of Kilkenny City, son of Anthony the younger son of Sir George, was captain in King James II's army, and died in 1695.

His two sons, Anthony and Mathew Saint Leger, went over to France in 1696, and became officers in the Irish Brigade of the French army. Anthony, captain-commandant of the Regiment of Bulkeley and Knight of St. Louis, died unmarried at St. Omer in Artois in 1747. Mathew, captain in the same body, was killed at the Battle of Culloden (April 1746), fighting in the ranks of the Young Pretender's army, and Richard de Saint Leger, his first cousin, captain in the Regiment of Rothe, lost his life at Fontenoy (May 1746).

Jean-Bertin de Saint Leger, eldest son of Mathew, was a captain in the Royal Scots, and a Knight of St. Louis. He received *'Confirmation de son ancienne noblesse'* by a sentence of the *Conseil de Etat* of Louis XVI at Versailles (21 June 1783). He suffered much in the French Revolution and died in 1794 leaving two sons. The first of these was Louis Justin Joseph, born in 1772, commandant du génie in the Imperial Army. He resigned in 1809. He was a Knight of St. Louis and a member of the Legion of Honour. He died unmarried in Paris in 1851.

His brother was Jean Jacques Maurice Saint Leger, born 1774, capitaine du génie in the Imperial Army. He also resigned in 1809, and died in Paris in 1861, leaving two sons. André Maurice de Saint Leger, his second son, born in 1802, was engineer-in-chief of the Corps Imperial des Mines, and an Officier of the Legion of Honour. He died in Paris in 1863, leaving one son and heir, Justin Maurice (1829-96), Knight of the Legion of Honour, Colonel of artillery, from whom the present line descends.

APPENDIX SIX

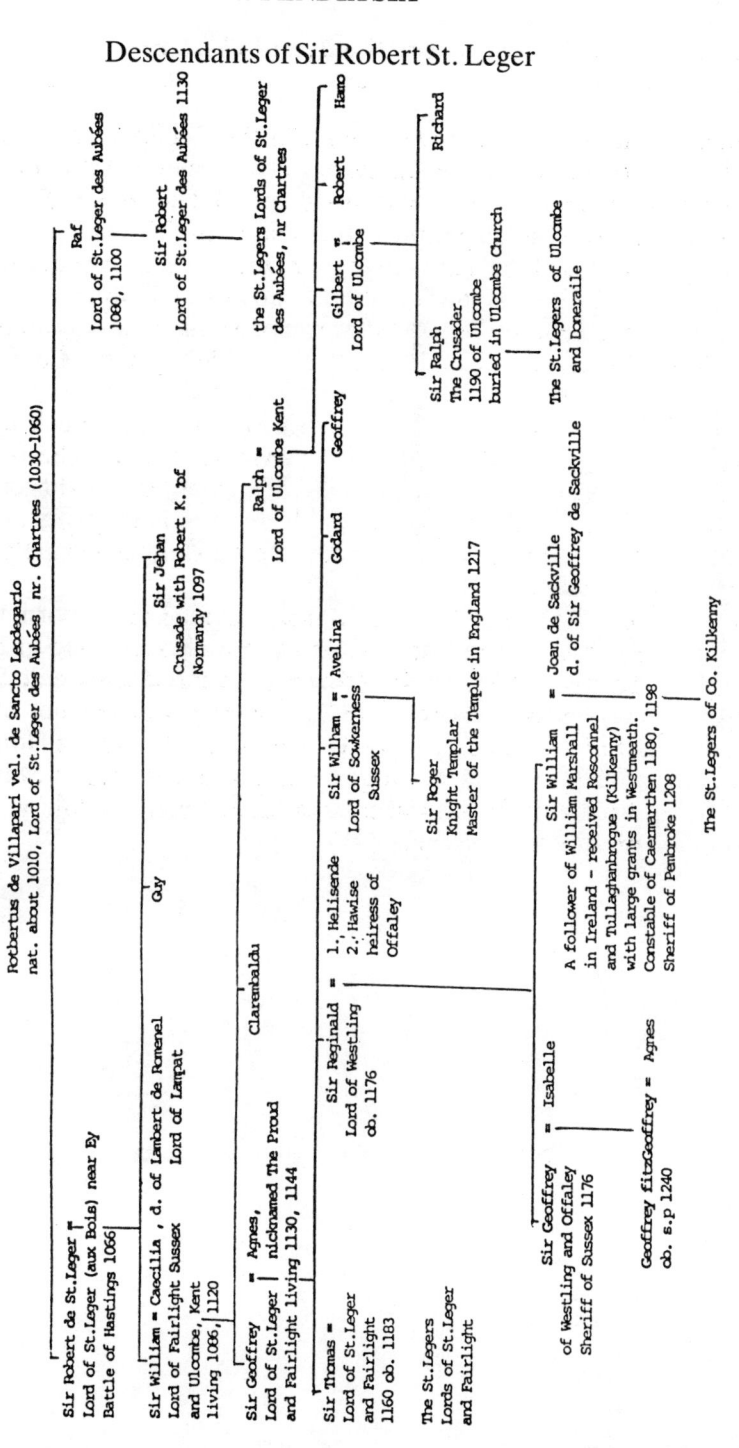

Descendants of Sir Robert St. Leger

Robertus de Villapari vel. de Sancto Leodegario
nat. about 1010, Lord of St.Leger des Aubées nr. Chartres (1030-1060)

- **Sir Robert de St.Leger**, Lord of St.Leger (aux Bois) near Ey, Battle of Hastings 1066
  - **Sir William** = Cecilia, d. of Lambert de Romenel, Lord of Lampat, Lord of Fairlight Sussex and Ulcombe, Kent, living 1066, 1120
    - **Sir Geoffrey** = Agnes, Lord of St.Leger, nicknamed The Proud, and Fairlight living 1130, 1144 | Clarembaldu
      - **Sir Thomas**, Lord of St.Leger and Fairlight 1160 ob. 1183
        - **Sir Reginald**, Lord of Westling ob. 1176 = 1. Helisende; 2. Hawise heiress of Offaley
          - The St.Legers Lords of St.Leger and Fairlight
      - **Sir William** = Avelina, Lord of Sookerness Sussex
        - **Sir Roger**, Knight Templar, Master of the Temple in England 1217
      - **Sir William** = Joan de Sackville, d. of Sir Geoffrey de Sackville
        A follower of William Marshall in Ireland – received Rosconnel and Tullaghanbrogue (Kilkenny) with large grants in Westmeath. Constable of Caermarthen 1180, 1198. Sheriff of Pembroke 1208
        - The St.Legers of Co. Kilkenny
      - **Sir Geoffrey** = Isabelle, of Westling and Offaley Sheriff of Sussex 1176
        - **Geoffrey fitzGeoffrey** = Agnes, ob. s.p 1240
  - **Guy**
    - **Sir Jehan**, Crusade with Robert K. of Normandy 1097
      - **Ralph** =, Lord of Ulcombe Kent
        - **Godard**
        - **Geoffrey**
        - **Gilbert** =, Lord of Ulcombe
          - **Sir Ralph**, The Crusader 1190 of Ulcombe buried in Ulcombe Church
          - **Robert**
          - **Richard**
          - The St.Legers of Ulcombe and Doneraile
        - **Hamo**
- **Raf**, Lord of St.Leger des Aubées 1060, 1100
  - **Sir Robert**, Lord of St.Leger des Aubées 1130
    - the St.Legers Lords of St.Leger des Aubées, nr Chartres

APPENDIX SEVEN

Some Descendants of the Lady Freemason

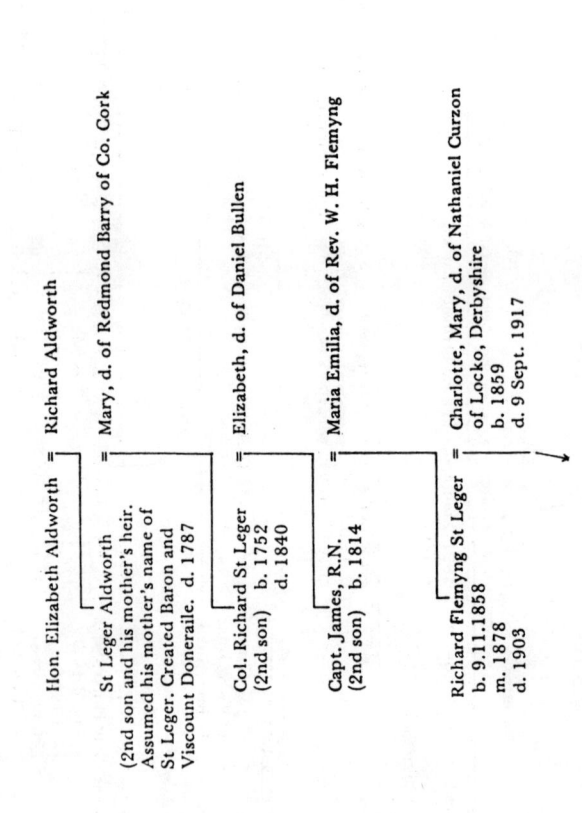

Hon. Elizabeth Aldworth = Richard Aldworth

St Leger Aldworth = Mary, d. of Redmond Barry of Co. Cork
(2nd son and his mother's heir.
Assumed his mother's name of
St Leger. Created Baron and
Viscount Doneraile. d. 1787

Col. Richard St Leger = Elizabeth, d. of Daniel Bullen
(2nd son) b. 1752
d. 1840

Capt. James, R.N. = Maria Emilia, d. of Rev. W. H. Flemyng
(2nd son) b. 1814

Richard Flemyng St Leger = Charlotte, Mary, d. of Nathaniel Curzon
b. 9.11.1858 of Locko, Derbyshire
m. 1878 b. 1859
d. 1903 d. 9 Sept. 1917

Major Charles Hayes St Leger-Curzon = 1. 1897, Louise, d. of M. de Bernis of Paris
b. 1879   d. 1899
Living in Paris and Monte Carlo
d. 3.5.1943
                                        = 2. Marie Louise, d. of Christian von Schleswig-Holstein-Sonderburg-Augustenburg
                                             b. 14.8.1872
                                             m. as his second wife in 1907 having previously been married herself
                                             d. 1957

Major Robert Hayes James St Leger = C. Joy Chantal Helene, d. of C. Charles Louis de Bourgogne
b. 9.1.1923   of Paris, Tours and Co. Cork
Sponsor: b. June, 1925
H.M. King Victor Emanuel of Italy
m. 1947

Captain Robert Hayes = Anne, d. of Major   Marc Philip Justin = C. Marie-Louise,   Charles Barry = Therese, d. of   Lindsay Joy = Desmond Brian Charles
Simon Aldworth   J. Digby, of   Onslow Berkeley   d. of D. de Brissac Warham   Col. Charles   Caroline   s. of Major William
b. 7.1.1948   Sherborne, Dorset   b. 3.6.1949   of Paris,   Montague   Gordon Lennox   b. 2.2.1960   Montagu Douglas Scott
                       b. 1947   Sponsor: H.R.H.   b. 19.2.1950   b. 27.5.1957   of Angus   m. July, 1977 b. May, 1959
                                            Prince Rupert of   killed in road   m. June, 1977   b. 10.10. 1960
                                            Bavaria and heir to accident
                                            the Marquis   15.10.1975
                                            St Leger
                                            m. 1.6.1969

         Justin Berkeley Domonic   Zoe Marina Joy   Lucy Charlotte   Elizabeth Ursula   Marie Joy Violet   Diana Eve Anne
         b. 16.2.1970   b. 25.6.1975   b. 15.1.1979   b. 1.7.1982   b. 1979   b. 1982
         killed 15.10.1975   killed 15.10.1975

                                   Christopher Neil   Charles Simon
                                   William   b. 1981
                                   b. 1978

St. Legers in Kent, 1619

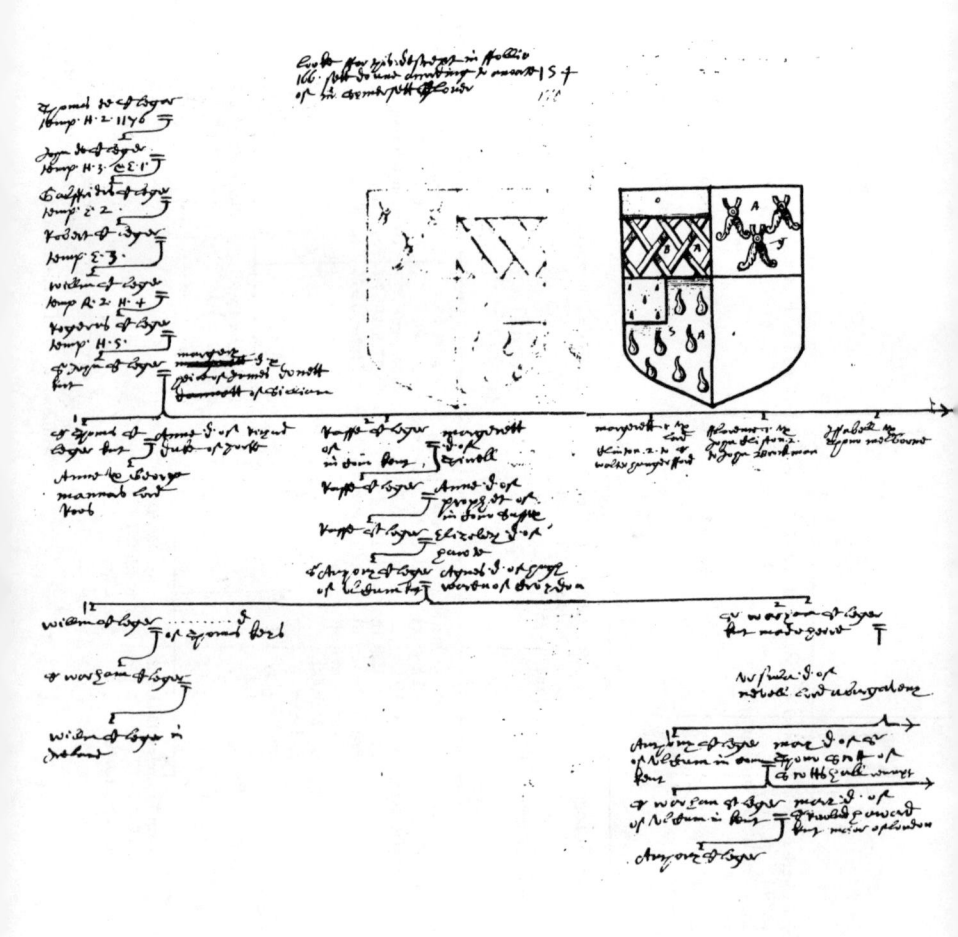

From the pedigree drawn up for the Heralds' Visitation of that year

Appendix Eight

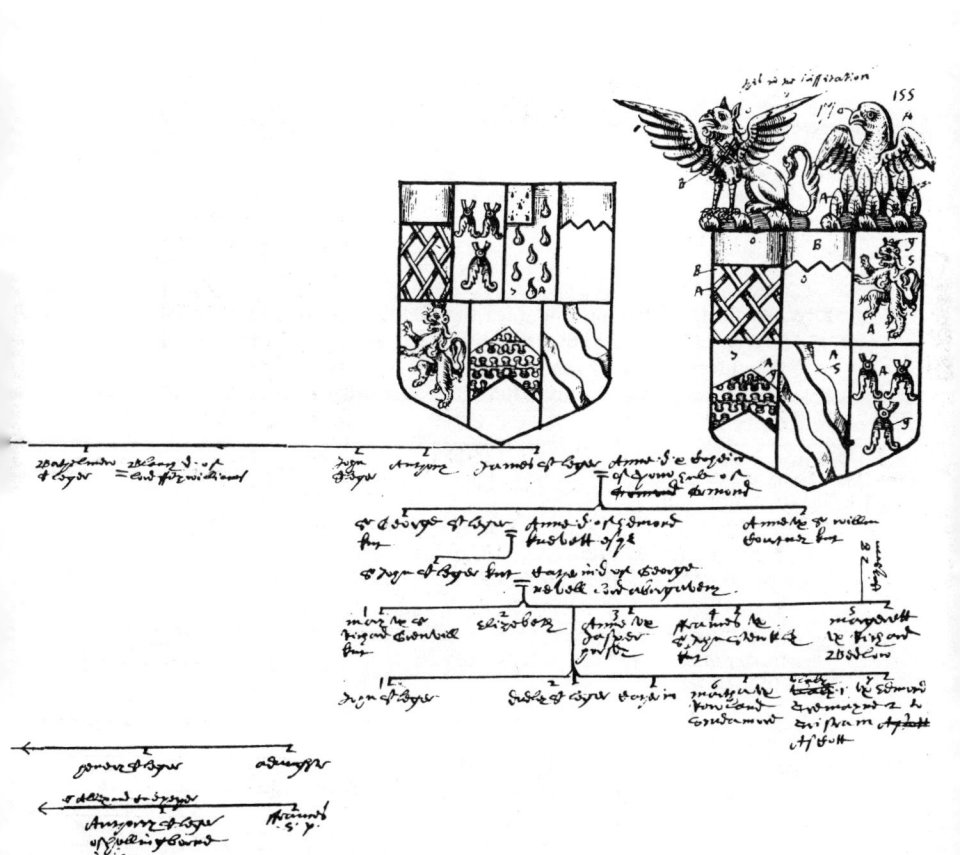

REFERENCES AND NOTES

Chapter One

1. Which Ralph is uncertain, since the Ralph mentioned here was married to Margaret Tyrrol, whereas his son, also Ralph, was the husband of Anne, daughter of John Prophete of Sussex.
2. *State Worthies*: David Lloyd (hereafter Lloyd).

Chapter Two

1. Lloyd, vol. I, p. 99
2. *The Works of Henry Howard, Earl of Surrey, and of Sir Thomas Wyatt the Elder*: edited by Frederick Nott, p. 45
3. *Calendar of State Papers Domestic: Henry VIII*, (hereafter CSPD HVIII) vol. 2, p. 452
4. *The Annuary of Kilkenny and the South-East of Ireland Archaeological Society*, Hore and Graves, pp. 124-36
5. CSPD HVIII, vol. 7, p. 532
6. Lloyd, p. 104
7. ibid, p. 102
8. *Dictionary of National Biography* (hereafter DNB), p. 652
9. *Calendar of State Papers: Ireland* (hereafter CSPI), vol. 1
10. Quoted in *The Peerage and Baronetage of the British Empire*, Lodge, pp. 99-100
11. DNB, p. 654
12. A Gaelic dagger
13. Lloyd, p. 101
14. CSPD HVIII, vol. 3, p. 285
15. *Historical Collections of the Church of Ireland during the Reigns of King Henry VIII, Edward VI and Queen Mary*, Robert Ware (London 1681): reprinted in the *Harleian Miscellany*, vol. 8, (1808-11) pp. 540-1
16. ibid, p. 601
17. *King Edward VI's Chronicle*, edited by W. K. Jordan, December 1551

18. Lord Conway
19. *History of Ireland*, Campion
20. *Chronicle of Ireland*, Holinshed
21. Quoted in *Athenae Cantabrigiensis*, p. 195
22. Lloyd, p. 104
23. *A History of Ireland*, E. Curtis (1936), p. 173
24. *Tudor and Stuart Ireland*, MacCurtain, p. 49

Chapter Three

1. CSPI (Elizabeth I), vol. 3
2. Public Record Office (hereafter PRO) Ref. State Papers 63/33, ff. 147-50
3. ibid, ff. 219-22
4. Harleian MSS, British Museum, Ref. 5M226634
5. Historical Manuscripts Commission, Salisbury MSS (Cecil Papers), Ref 13/13
6. The fact that two St. Legers, separated by a generation, were associated with Sir Walter Raleigh, is demonstrated by these dates: Raleigh was born in 1552 and died in 1618; Sir Warham St. Leger I was born in 1525 and died in 1597 and Sir Warham St. Leger II was born around 1575 and died in 1631.
7. *Works*, Sir Walter Raleigh, vol. 1, p. 482, vol. 8, p 634
8. *Annals of the Coinage of Britain*, Rogers Ruding, vol. 2, p. 319
9. ibid
10. *The Mint*, Sir John Craig, p. 171
11. *The History of Deal*, Pritchard, p. 141

Chapter Four

1. 'Doneraile Castle and Court', James Grove White, *Journal of the Cork Historical and Archaeological Society* (hereafter White), 1913, p. 43
2. *Bowens Court*, Elizabeth Bowen, p. 55
3. Lord Muskerry is known in Irish history as MacCarthy Mor
4. After being expelled from the Dublin Parliament, the Roman Catholic party formed the Catholic Confederacy of Kilkenny in October 1642 to represent its interests. The confederates pledged themselves to the establishment of the Catholic Church in Ireland, to the restitution of lands confiscated for 'religion' (notably abbey lands), and to liberty of trade as well as to the independence of the Irish Parliament. They were not anti-royalist, their motto being '*Pro Deo, pro Rege, pro Patria Hibernia unanimis*' (Ireland united for God, King and Country).
5. White, p. 46
6. ibid
7. ibid
8. This detail does not tally with the house as it stands today
9. *Memoir of the Lady Freemason*, Brother John Day, p. 12
10. ibid, p. 12

11. ibid, p. 15
12. I am indebted to Callaghan O'Callaghan for this information
13. ibid

Chapter Five

1. Roger Longrigg tells me that an 18th-century Yorkshire landowner would be more likely to have a private racecourse than not. Private racing was widespread then, particularly in Yorkshire.
2. The Doncaster Race Club Committee, 1776

Chapter Six

1. *Clubs of the Georgian Rakes*, Louis C. Jones, pp. 82-3
2. One of the many details supplied to me by the Firbeck History Group

Chapter Seven

1. *The Expedition of Lieutenant-Colonel Barry St. Leger*, p. 155
2. ibid, pp. 169-170
3. Major-General G. B. Mundy, *The Life of Admiral Rodney* (1830), as quoted in *St. Lucia*, H. Breen, pp. 70-1
4. ibid
5. ibid

Chapter Eight

1. *Poems*, Barry St. Leger, p. 9
2. ibid, p. 51
3. *The Bohemian*, Barry St. Leger
4. ibid, p. 177
5. ibid, p. 299
6. ibid, p. 31
7. ibid, p. 134
8. ibid, p. 219
9. *The Annual Biography and Obituary of Celebrated Persons*, 1829
10. ibid
11. *Poems*, Barry St. Leger, p. 72
12. ibid, p. 23

Chapter Nine

1. *Cape Times*, 1 July 1882
2. *Cape Times*, editorial
3. *Cape Times*, 29 March 1881
4. *An Editor Looks Back*, G. A. L. Green

5. ibid, p. 42
6. The cemetery was cleared in 1976 to make way for a playing field, but a memorial door to Frederick York St. Leger in the church will be sculpted by the South African artist Bill Davis.
7. *Some Beginnings*, Gerald Shaw, p. 58
8. ibid, pp. 122-3

Chapter Ten

1. *Skeleton Reef*, Hugh St. Leger, p. 15
2. Private letter from Mrs. Eigen Ramsay Murray, 1976

BIBLIOGRAPHY

Manuscript Sources

British Museum Harleian Manuscript Collection; Cotton Manuscripts, Titus B, xiii
Historical Manuscripts Commission, Manuscripts of the Marquess of Salisbury (Cecil Papers)

Published Sources

Edward Hasted, *The History and Topographical Survey of Kent* (Ed. 1972)
J. A. Gaughan, *Doneraile* (Kamac Publications, 1970)
Helen Cam, *England before Elizabeth* (Grey Arrow Books, 1961)
P. Holohan, *Ireland* (The Educational Company of Ireland, 1973)
M. E. Collins, *Ireland 1800-1970* (Longman, 1976)
Gerald Shaw, *Some Beginnings* (Oxford University Press, 1975)
E. H. Carter and R. A. Mears, *The History of Britain*, vol. 1 (Oxford University Press, 1937)
A. Laker, *History of Deal* (1950)
W. K. Jordan (ed.), *The Chronicle and Political Papers of Edward VI* (1966)
George Frederick Nott, *The Works of Henry Howard, Earl of Surrey, and of Sir Thomas Wyatt the Elder* (London, 1815)
Barry St. Leger, *Tales of Passion* (Henry Colburn, 1829)
Athenae Cantabrigienses
J. Lodge (ed.), *The Peerage and Baronetage of the British Empire* (1881)
Dictionary of National Biography
B. Tomlinson, *Doncaster from the Roman Occupation* (1900)
William Sheardown, *Historical Notices of Doncaster Races* (1861)
Roger Mortimer, *The Jockey Club* (Cassell, 1958)
J. Fairfax-Blakeborough, *Northern Turf History* (J. A. Allen, 1950)
David Hunn, *Epsom Racecourse* (Davis Poynter, 1973)

Bibliography

A. C. Fryer, *Wooden Monumental Effigies in England and Wales* (1924)
J. S. Fletcher, *History of the St. Leger Stakes* (Hutchinson, 1939)
Burke's *Dictionary of the Landed Gentry*
John Nichols, *History and Antiquities of the County of Leicester*, vol. 3 (1800)
G. Marshall, *The Genealogist's Guide* (Heraldry Today, 1973)
Barry St. Leger, *Remorse and other Poems* (1821)
Paul Kendall, *Richard the Third* (Allen and Unwin, 1955)
Cora Schofield, *The Life and Reign of Edward IV* (Frank Cass Reprints, 1967)
A. Ellis, *Three Hundred Years of London's River* (1965)
Thomas Fuller, *Worthies of England* (Allen and Unwin, 1952)
J. Dallaway, *Sussex* (1810)
W. J. Hocking, *Catalogue of the Royal Mint Museum* (1977)
Sir John Craig, *The Mint* (1956)
Revd. Rogers Ruding, *Annals of the Coinage of Britain* (1867)
G. R. Corner, *History of Horsely Down* (1858)
E. Rendle, *Old Southwark and its People* (1878)
F. J. Snell, *Devonshire: Historical – Descriptive* (1907)
County Genealogies: Pedigrees of the Families of Kent
Daniel and Samuel Lysons, *Magna Britannia* (1822)
J. L. Vivian (ed.), *Visitations of the Counties of Devon* (1895)
John Prince, *The Worthies of Devon* (1810)
An Elizabethan Virginal Book
Charles Wykeham-Martin, *Leeds Castle* (1869)
Sir Walter Raleigh, *Works* (1618)
Louis C. Jones, *Clubs of the Georgian Rakes* (1942)
The Annual Biography and Obituary of Celebrated Persons (Longman, 1830)
Elizabeth Bowen, *Bowens Court* (Longmans, 1956)
William Henry Curran, *The Life of John Philpot Curran* (London, 1819)
Brother John Day, *Memoir of the Honorable Elizabeth Aldworth, the Lady Freemason* (repr. Cork, 1941)
F. Hore & G. Graves (eds.), *The Annuary of the Kilkenny and South-East of Ireland Archaeological Society* (1910)
G. A. L. Green, *An Editor Looks Back* (1947)
W. L. Stone, *The Campaign of Lt. Gen. John Burgoyne and the Expedition of Lt. Col. Barry St. Leger* (Munsell, 1877)
H. H. Breen, *St. Lucia: Historical, Statistical and Descriptive* (1844)
I. Parry and J. Sherlock, *A Short History of the West Indies* (Macmillan, 1963)
Robert Ware (ed.), *Historical Collections of the Church of Ireland, during the Reigns of Henry VIII, Edward VI and Queen Mary* (1681, reprinted *Harleian Miscellany*, vol. 8, 1810)
J. Holinshed, *Chronicle of Ireland* (1604)
Calendar of State Papers, PRO Ref. 63/33 ff. 147-150, ff. 219-22
Acts of the Privy Council
Calendar of State Papers Domestic: Henry VIII
Gordon Home, *Epsom Racecourse* (1961)

Victoria County History of Surrey
Major-General G. B. Mundy, *The Life of Admiral Rodney* (John Murray, 1830)

Articles, Pamphlets, Journals

Sussex Archaeological Collections, vol. 7
Lord Geoffrey Lloyd, *Leeds Castle* (Leeds Castle Foundation, 1962)
Richard Stone, 'Ulcombe, Ireland and the St. Legers', *Archaeologia Cantiana*, vol. 91 (1976)
Harry Blackburne and Maurice Bond, *The Romance of St. George's Chapel, Windsor Castle* (1976)
Shelagh Bond, *St. George's Chapel* (1974)
Annual Report of the Society of Friends of St. George's (1968)
James Grove White, 'Doneraile Castle and Court', *Journal of the Cork Archaeological and Historical Society* (1913)
Anthony St. Leger: The Founder of Modern Racing (Doncaster Racecard of 1976)

INDEX

Abergavenny, *see* Neville
Acre, 2
Act of Union, 53
Aldworth, Richard, 47
Aldworth, St. Leger, 48
Alen, John, 19
Allabaculia, 64
America, 58
American War of Independence, 64, Chapter Seven
Anglican Church, 93, 103
Anne of Cleves, 14
Annery, 7, 8, 126
Antilles, 89
Archbishop of Canterbury, 2, 12
Archer, Fred, 69
Arms, 125
Arnold, General, 86
Arscott, Tristan, 8
Awbeg, R., 39, 45

Baillie, Lady Olive, 23
Bahram, 69
Ballyally, 101
Ballyclough, 52
Barbados, 89
Battle Abbey Roll, 126
Batty, 81
Bell Brothers, 71
Bellingham, Sir Edward, 20
Belloc, Hilaire, 6
Bentinck, Lord George, 68
Berni Inns, 72
Bexhill, 1
Boer War, 104, 106
Boleyn, Sir William, 7
Boleyn, Anne, 7, 8, 10, 23
Bosworth, Battle of, 7
Bottesford, 7
Bouillé, Marquis de, 90
Boulogne, 18, 19
Boyle, 42
Brabazon, Sir William, 20
Browne, George, 21, 22

Brussels, 14
Buckingham, Duke of, 5
Buckingham Palace, 79
Buckinghamshire, 79
Buckle, Frank, 69
Bunbury, Sir Charles, 87
Burgoyne, General, 83, 85, 97, 98
Butler, *see* Ormonde
Butler, Anne, 7
Butler, Eleanor, 5
Butler, Margaret, 7
Buttevant, 51, 52
Byrd, William, 8
Byron, Lord, 98

Caerlaverock, Battle of, 3
Cambridge, 77, 109
Canada, 83-6
Canterbury, 11, 12, 109
Cantley Common, 63, 65
Caribbean, 79, 88, 91
Carlow, 15, 18
Carr, John, 65
Carrickfergus Castle, 41
Carrickline, 34
Castlehaven, Lord, 43
Castletown, Lord, 53, 54
Castletown, Lady Ursula, 53
Castries Bay, 90
Catterson, Olga, 71
Cape Argus, 105
Cape Colony, 105
Cape Parliament, 106
Cape Times, 104-6
Capetown, 102, 104, 106
Cavendish, William, 11
Charles I, 35, 41, 58
Charles II, 35
Charles V, Emperor, 14, 23
Chester, Harriet, 80
Chester, John, 80
Christian Brothers, 54
Church of Christ, Canterbury, 11, 22, 126

Church of the Province, 103
Colenso, Bishop, 103
Coleridge, Samuel Taylor, 98
College of Arms, 125, 126
Cooke, Joan, 71
Cornwall, 109
Cork, 13, 18, 34, 36, 39, 50
Cork City, 40, 43, 44
Corpus Christi College, 101
Coulter, Edward, 56
Cotterill, Bishop, 102
Cox, Don, 72, 74
Cox, Sir Richard, 45
Cranmer, Archbishop Thomas, 11
Cromwell, Oliver, 43, 58
Cromwell, Thomas, 10, 14
Crow, 72
Crusades, 2
Culpepper, Sir Thomas, 35
Curran, John Philpot, 49-50

Dayan, Moshe, 23
Deal, 36, 37
Derby, 66, 69, 73, 87, 88
Derby, 11th Earl of, 87
Derby, 12th Earl of, 87
Desmond, James Fitzjohn Fitzgerald, 16, 19, 30-2
Destiny, 34
Deutsches St. Leger, 72
Devon, 7, 8, 80, 126
Diamond Jubilee, 69
Digby, Elizabeth, 7
Digby, Thomas, 7
Digges, Sir Thomas, 34
Dissolution of the Monasteries, 10, 11
Domesday Book, 2
Dominica, 89, 91
Doncaster, Chapter Five, 77, 78, 88
Doncaster Race Meeting, Chapter Five
Doncaster, Mansion House, 65, 66
Doncaster, Town Moor, 65
Doneraile, Chapter Four
Doneraile, Viscounts, 51

Doneraile Baptismal Suit, 51-2
Doneraile Castle, 39, 40, 41, 43
Doneraile Catholic Church, 53
Doneraile Court, 39, 45-6, 54, 56-9
Doneraile legends, 54-6
Doneraile Park, 39, 46, 55
Doneraile Presentation Convent, 53
Doneraile school, 54
Dortmund, 52
Drogheda, 13, 43
Drummer, The, 63
Dublin, 13, 15, 16, 18, 20, 21, 58, 79, 80
Düsseldorf, 14
Dunfermline, 70
Dungarvan Castle, 20

East India Company, 102
Edward, Prince in the Tower, 5
Edward, Prince of Wales, 69, 70
Edward I, 3
Edward III, 3
Edward IV, 4
Edward VI, 20, 22, 23, 24
Edward VII, 45
Elis, 68
Elizabeth I, 3, 29, 30, 33, 35
Elizabeth II, 70
Elnothington, Manor of, 3
English liturgy, 20-1
Epsom, 87, 88
Eton, 77
Exeter, 5

Fermanagh, Maguire, Lord of, 40
Feudal system, 3, 93
Firbeck, 63, 71, 78, 81
Fitzgerald, Sir John, 30-2
Fitzpatrick, Tom, 59
Fitzwilliam, Lord, 70
Fitzwilliam, Sir William, 25
Flatman, Nat, 69
Flores, Battle of, 8
Flying Dutchman, 69
Flying Fox, 69

Index

Fort Royal, 90, 91
Fort Schuyler, 84-6
France, 19, 72, 79, 89

Gainsborough, 79
Gainsborough, race horse, 69
Gallimore, 71
Gally Knight family, 81
Garrett, Edmund, 107
Garter King of Arms, 9
Garter, Knights of, 22, 24
Garter, Order of the, 18
Gentry, 93
George IV (*see* Prince of Wales)
George VI, 70
Georgian Society of Ireland, 38, 58, 59
Gladiateur, 69
Gladstone, 105
Goldwell, Emeline, 34
Goodwood, 68
Graham, T. L., 107
Grahamstown, 102, 103
Grasse, Comte de, 90, 91
Gratton, 53
Gray, Bishop, 102
Great Rebellion, 41-2
Green, General, 88
Green, G. A. L., 105, 106
Grenville, Sir Richard, 8
Grey, Lady Jane, 29
Grimsby, 78
Guiana, 34, 44
Guilford, Lord, 94

Handsome Jack, (*see* John Hayes St. Leger)
Hannah, 69
Hales, Sir Christopher, 11
Hastings, Battle of, 1
Hapsburg, Emperor Charles V, 14, 23
Hell Fire Club, 80
Henry II, 2
Henry III, 2
Henry VI, 126

Henry VII, 5, 7
Henry VIII, 6, 7, 8, Chapter Two
Herald's Office, 25, 125, 126
Heyward, Mary, 34
Heyward, Sir Rowland, 34
Heyward's Hill, 44, 126
Hollingbourne, 3
Holy Land, 2
Hood, Admiral, 90, 91
Horse Racing, Chapter Five
Horsmanden, Daniel, 36
House of Commons, 87
House of Lords, 57

Inchiquin, Baron, 17
Inchiquin, Lord, 43
India, 94, 109
Innes, James Rose, 106
Ireland, Chapters Two-Four, 2, 8, 91, 101, 111
Irish Land Commission, 58
Irish Parliament, 12, 16, 17, 18, 53
Irish Privy Council, 29, 40
Isinglass, 69

Jackson, John, 70
Jamaica, 89
James I, 40
Jameson Raid, 105
Jebb family, 81
Jenkins, Roy, 23
Jockey Club, 64, 78, 87
John, King, 2
John, Edith, 71

Kamel, Muhammed, 23
Kavanagh, 15
Keats, John, 98
Kemble, 94
Kent, 1, 3, 4, 29, 35, 126
Kent, Grand Jury of, 8, 10
Kent, Knights of, 2, 129
Kent, Sheriffs of, 2, 129

Kilcolman, 41
Kildare, 18, 77
Kildorrery, 42
Kilkenny, 13
Kilmallock, 16
Kimberley, 103
King's Court, 3

Lagrange, Comte de, 69
Lancashire, 68
Lancaster Herald, 9
Laughton, Manor of, 78
Leeds Castle, 4, 22-3, 29, 30, 31, 33, 35
Leeds Priory, 11
Leicester, Lord, 32
Leicestershire, 7
Leinster, 2
Leix, 20, 40
Letwell, 81
Limerick, 16, 18, 40, 101
Liversidge, Winifred, 73
London, 29, 30, 31, 68, 87, 88, 94, 101
London, Tower of, 30
Louis XI, 4
Louis XVI, 79
Louth, 13

MacGillpatrick of Ossory, 16
MacWilliam of Connaught, 16
Madras, 109
Maguire (*see* Fermanagh)
Majuba, 105
Maidstone, 12
Mallow, 39
Manchester, 68
Manners, George, Lord Ros, 6
Maria, Queen of Hungary, 14
Marlborough, Duke of, 36
Martinique, 90
Meath, 13
Melba, Dame Nellie, 109
Memnon, 68
Midland News, 107
More, Sir Thomas, 22

Monkleigh Church, 8
Monmouthshire, 101
Montgarret, Lord, 42
Muddle, Christian Emma, 102
Muddle, John, 102
Munster, 16, 18, 29, 30, 32, 33, 40
Muskerry, Lord, 42-3

Natal, 102
Neil, Father, 49
Netherlands, 14, 37, 40
Neville, Catherine, 9
Neville, George, Lord Abergavenny, 9, 33
Neville, Ursula, 9, 33
Newbury, Second Battle of, 43
Newmarket, 64, 68
New Zealand, 56
Nijinsky, 69
Normans, 1, 2, 12, 13
Nutwith, 68

Oaks, The, 87, 89

O'Brien, clan chief, 16, 17
O'Brien, Very Rev., 53
O'Byrne, clan, 20
O'Callaghan, Callaghan, 59, 60
O'Carroll of Ely, Baron, 19
O'Connor, clan, 15, 19, 20
O'Donnell, clan chief, 17
Oettingen-Wallerstein, Countess, 72
Offaly, 20, 40
Okehampton, 80
Old Saint (*see* Frederick York St. Leger)
O'More, clan chief, 15, 20
O'Neill, clan chief, 17
Ontario, 83
Ormonde, Thomas Butler, 7th Earl of, 7
Ormonde, James Butler, 9th Earl of, 19
Ormonde, Thomas Butler, 10th Earl of, 30
Ormonde, James Butler, 12th Earl of, 43
Ormonde, race horse, 69

Index

Oronoko, river, 35
Orville, 69
O'Toole, clan, 15
Oundle School, 101

Pale, The, 13, 18, 29
Paris, 52
Park Hill, 63, 71, Chapter Six
Park Hill Stakes, 78
Parkhurst, Sir William, 35
Parliament, 3, 41, 43
Pasteur, Louis, 52
Pearce, Jim, 72
Perrott, Sir John, 30

Persimmon, 69
Peterhouse, Cambridge, 77
Petre, The Hon. E., 70
Pevensey, 1
Piggott, Lester, 69
Plantagenet, Anne, Duchess of Exeter, 4
Plantagenet arms, 5
Plymouth, 36
Portsmouth, 36
Poteyn, Juliana, 3
P. & O. Company, 101
Princes in the Tower, 5
Prince of Wales, 79, 80
Privy Chamber, 7, 14, 22
Privy Council, 12, 19, 22, 25, 30, 31
Punch, 111

Queen's County, 40
Queenstown, 102

Raleigh, Sir Walter, 32, 34, 44
Rathcooney, 44
Red Lion Inn, 63, 71, 72, 74
Rees, John ap, 11
Remembrancer, 70
Revenge, The, 8
Reynolds, Sir Joshua, 79
Rhodes, Cecil, 104, 105, 110

Rich, Sir Richard, 11
Richard I, 2
Richard, Duke of Gloucester, 4, 5
Richard, Duke of York, 5
Richards, Sir Gordon, 69
Rochester, 36
Rockingham, Lord, 64, 65, 87
Rodney, Admiral, 90, 91
Rome, 32
Roman Catholicism, 21, 22, 24
Roper, William, 22
Ros tomb, 6
Rothery, 45
Rothschild, Baron de, 69
Royal Mint, The, 35
Royal Navy, 89, 90, 91
Rugby School, 94
Rutland Chapel, Windsor, 5, 6
Rutland, Thomas 1st Duke of (*temp.* Henry VIII), 6
Rutland, Duke and Duchess of (*temp.* George III), 80

St. Andrew's College, Grahamstown, S. A., 102
St. Augustine's Inn, Southwark, 11, 30
St. Augustine's Priory, Canterbury, 11, 30
St. Finbarre's Cathedral, Cork, 48
St. George's Chapel, Windsor, 5, 6, 126
St. Lawrence, river, 83
St. Leger, general: arms, 5, 126; chantry (Windsor), 5, 6; – House, Southwark, 30, 31; – Stakes, Chapter Five, 87, 88; – Race Bicentenary, 70-2; tapestry, 71;
St. Leger, family: Anne, Duchess of Exeter, 4, 126; Anne, Lady Ros, 6; Anne, 4; Anne, 34; Arnuld, 3; Sir Anthony of Bottesford, 6; Sir Anthony, K. G., 4, Chapter Two, 127, 129, 130; Sir Anthony, 7; Sir Anthony, Warden of the Mint, 35-6; Sir Anthony, 33; Anthony, 33;

Anthony Butler, 80; Anthony Francis, 80; Anthony, Major General, 63, 65, 66, 77-9, 87, 88, 91, 130; Arthur, 11; Arthur, Baron Kilmayden and 1st Viscount Doneraile, 46, 77; Arthur, 109; Barbara, 44; Barry, Major, 83-6, 88; Bonfoy, Major, 81; David, 127; Dudley, 36; Dudley, son of, 36; Edward, Dr., 36-7; Edward, 6th Viscount Doneraile, 53, 57, 58; Eigen Ramsay Murray, 111; Elizabeth, 46-8; Emma, 103; Francis Barry Boyle, Chapter Eight; Frederick York, Chapter Nine, 109, 127; Sir George, 8, 129; George, 12, 33; Gertrude de Vries, 40; Hayes, 4th Viscount Doneraile, 46, 48; Hayes, 2nd Viscount Doneraile, (2nd creation), 130; Hayes, 4th Viscount Doneraile, (2nd creation), 52-3; Hayes, Captain, 88; Heyward, Lt. Colonel, 36, 44; Hugh, 7th Viscount Doneraile, 56, 57, 127; Sir Hugh, 109, 110; Isabel, 9; Sir James, 7; Jane, 44; Sir John, 2; Sir John, Sheriff of Kent, 126, 129; Sir John of Annery, 8, 9, 129; Sir John of Grangemellan, 77; John, 46; John Chester, 80-1; John Hayes, 79-80, 130; Julian, 70; Malcolm, Rear-Admiral St. Leger Searle, 103; Marion, 106; Mary Grenville, 8; Mary Heyward, 34; Mary, 56, 57; Sir Ralph, the Crusader, 2; Sir Ralph (2), 129; Sir Ralph, Sheriff of Kent, 129, 130; Sir Ralph, Sheriff of Kent, 129; Sir Ralph, 2; Sir Ralph, 3, 130; Ralph, Sheriff of Kent, 4, 126, 129; Richard, 8th Viscount Doneraile, 57, 59; Richard St. John, 57, 58; Sir Robert, 1, 2, 125, 128; Robert, 20; Robert, 101; Rowland, 36; Rupert, 109; St. Leger, 1st Viscount Doneraile, (2nd creation), 48, 49-51, 54; Sir Thomas, 2; Sir Thomas, Sheriff of Kent, 129; Sir Thomas, 4, 5, 36, 126, 129; Sir Thomas FitzAnthony, 2; Sir Thomas of Otterden, 3; Ursula, 33; Ursula, Lady Castletown, 53; Walter of Carrickline, 34; Sir Warham I, 10, 12, 29-33, 129; Sir Warham II, 34; Sir Warham III, 40; Warham, 109; Sir William, Sheriff of Kent, 129; Sir William, 40-3; Sir William, 43; William, 12, 29, 40; William, 109; William Nassau, 101, 109

Sellinger's Round, 8
St. Lucia, 79, 88-91
St. Mary's Church, Slindon, 6
St. Mary's Church, Battle, 125
St. Mary le Tower, Ipswich, 101
St. Michael's Church, Queenstown, S. A., 102
St. Patrick's Cathedral, Dublin, 16
St. Paul's School, 101
St. Thomas' Church, Rondebosch, S. A., 106
Saint-Martin, Yves, 72
Salisbury, 5
Saratoga, battle of, 86
Scotland, 29, 41
Scott, Sir Walter, 98
Scott, William, 69
Shannon, river, 17
Shaw, Gerald, 106
Shelley, Percy Bysshe, 98
Sheridan, Richard Brinsley, 94
Sidney, Sir Henry, 29
Sinclair, Francis, 71
Singleton, John, 64
Slindon, 6
Smirke, Charlie, 69
Smith, Benjamin, 70
Smith, 'Customer', 35
Smith, Sir Richard, 35
Somerset, Duke of, 20, 29
Somerville, Rev., 51

Index

South Africa, Chapter Nine
Spain, 8, 32, 89
Spanish Succession, Wars of, 36
Spenser, Sylvanus, 41
Sprigg, Sir Gordon, 106
Stanley, Lady Charlotte, 87
Stephens, Margaret, 71
Sussex, 6
Sweepstakes, 64
Sidney, Sir Philip, 46
Synan family, 39, 41

Thanet, 36
Thayendanegea, Chief, 83, 85
Theodore, 70
Thomond, O'Brien, Earl of, 17, 19
Thunder, 34
Tipperary, 13
Transvaal, 105
Treaty of Versailles, 91
Trincomalee, 80
Triple Crown, 69
Town Moor, 65, 70, 73, 87
Tudor, Henry, 10
Tudor, Mary, 24, 29
Two Thousand Guineas, 66, 69
Tyrone, O'Neill, Earl of, 17, 19

Ulcombe, 1, 2, 4, 10, 12
Ulcombe Church, 2, 126
Ulcombe Manor, 2, 23, 25, 29, 33, 35
Ulster, 41
Upper Ossory, Barons of, 19

Vance, Cyrus, 23
Victoria, Princess, 70
Vries, Gertrude van de, 40

Waddesdon Manor, 79
Warham, William, Archbishop of
    Canterbury, 12, 22
Waterford, 13, 20
Watson-Wentworth, Charles, 2nd
    Marquis of Rockingham, 64

Wentworth, 41
West Australian, 69
West Indies, 88-91
Westminster Abbey, 5
Weston, Tommy, 69
Wexford, 13, 18, 43
Whaley, Mr., 79
Wildenstein, Mr., 72
Wilkinson, Tate, 78
William IV, 70
William the Conqueror, 1
Wimbledon, 53
Wolsey, Cardinal, 7, 10
Wombwell, Margaret, 77
Woodville, Elizabeth, 5
Woodville Rebellion, 5
Worksop, 63, 78,
Wyatt, Sir Thomas, 10
Wyatt, Sir Thomas the Younger, 29

York Race Meeting, 67
Yorkshire, 68, 78, 80